Change Management for Semantic Web Services

Xumin Liu • Salman Akram
Athman Bouguettaya

Change Management for Semantic Web Services

Foreword by Michael P. Papazoglou

Springer

Xumin Liu
Rochester Institute of
Technology
Department of Computer Science
Lomb Memorial Drive 102
14623 Rochester
USA
xl@cs.rit.edu

Athman Bouguettaya
CSIRO ICT Center
CS & IT Building (108)
North Road
2601 Acton, ACT
Australia
athman.bouguettaya@csiro.au

Salman Akram
The George Washington
University
Department of Information
Technology
Knoll Square 44983
20147 Ashburn Virginia
USA
msakram@gmail.com

ISBN 978-1-4899-9991-7   ISBN 978-1-4419-9329-8 (eBook)
DOI 10.1007/978-1-4419-9329-8
Springer New York Dordrecht Heidelberg London

To my husband Qi and my daughter Emily for their love, encouragement, and support.

Xumin Liu

To my wife, Sameera, and my daughter, Aizah.

Salman Akram

To my wife Malika and my three children Zakaria, Ayoub, and Mohamed-Islam.

Athman Bouguettaya

Foreword

Software automates a wide variety of business processes in modern enterprises. Changes made to software are, in effect, changes made to the business processes themselves that govern and automate the internal and external operations of an organization. Without a proper disciplined approach to change management, enterprises lack a full understanding of how software running in production can help them automate their business processes. This includes management of changes to software in development, changes to software in production, and changes to associated artifacts like requirements, models, and test cases. It also includes management of both individual changes and the coordination of dependent changes.

According to ITIL v3, which is the most widely adopted approach for IT Service Management, the purpose of Change Management is to ensure that standardized methods are used for the efficient and prompt handling and recording of all changes so that the overall impact of software changes and business risk is minimized. Change Management is all about ensuring that software changes are recorded, evaluated, authorized, prioritized, planned, tested, implemented, documented and reviewed in a controlled manner.

The past few years saw an increased use of reusable services as a means for the development of business critical applications. The software application is not programmed from scratch but rather assembled using a variety of reusable software services. In an environment of constant change and variation driven by competition and innovation, a software service can rarely remain stable. Consequently, the service-based application development trajectory sets exceptional requirements and challenges for change management. These include, for example, predicting the impact of changes, analyzing the compatibility of service versions which are part of service compositions, preventing changes that result in spurious and uncontrolled service behavior, preventing changes from spilling over a versioned service to other associated services, coordinating the management of dependent changes, and so forth. Alternatively corporate compliance and market trends may force an organization to remove or replace possibly outsourced software services (as in the cloud) that meet the new requirements.

Services typically evolve by accommodating a multitude of changes (beyond the creation or decommissioning of a service) along the following, non-mutually exclusive dimensions:

1. Structural changes, which focus on changes that occur on the service data types, messages and operations, collectively known as service signatures.
2. Behavioral changes that affect the behavior and the business protocol of a service. Behavioral changes concentrate on analyzing the spreading effects of changing service operations. If, for example, we consider an order management service we might expect to see a service that lists "place order", "cancel-order," and "update order," and so on, as available operations. Assume now that the "update-order" operation is modified in such a way that it includes "available-to-promise" functionality, which dynamically allocates and reallocates resources to promise and fulfill customer orders. The modified operation must guarantee that if part of the order is outsourced to a manufacturing partner, this partner can fulfill its order on time to meet agreed upon shipment dates and conditions. This requires, among other things, understanding of where time is consumed in the manufacturing process, what is "normal" with respect to an events timeliness with as regards the deadline, and to understand standard deviations with respect to that manufacturing process events and on-time performance. Business protocols, on the other hand, specify the external messaging and perceived behavior of services (viz. the rules that govern the service interaction between service providers and consumers) and, in particular, the conversations that the services can participate in.
3. Policy-induced changes describe changes in policy assertions and constraints on the invocation of the service. For instance, they express changes to the Quality of Service(QoS) characteristics and compliance requirements of a service.

The evolution of services is expressed through the creation and decommissioning of different service versions during its lifetime. These versions have to be aligned with each other in a non-disruptive manner and in a way that would allow a service designer to track the various modifications and their effects on the service. To control service evolution therefore, a designer needs to know why a change was made, what its implications are, and whether the change is consistent. Eliminating spurious results and inconsistencies that may occur due to uncontrolled changes is thus a necessity for services to evolve gracefully, ensure service stability, and handling variability in their behavior. The general idea is that services should be designed to respond in a safe, proportionate manner when erroneous or unexpected changes occur. In this way, changes and enhancements can be made to individual services and released as new versions without causing an impact on the existing applications and services that consume the new service version. In many circumstances it also desirable to keep many versions of the same service "alive".

This book deals with service management, which is a notoriously complex topic in a very sound and intuitive manner. It addresses the most important problems providing a mixture of theoretical and practical solutions in the context of end-to-end framework that deals with different types of changes. It is interesting to note that the proposed change strategies are embodied in and managed by a so called service change schema whose purpose is to control and delimit changes. This allows a structured and disciplined approach to handling service changes. In addition, a set of rules is introduced to determine the correctness of the topology of a service change schema. These rules are used as the guidance to verify the correctness of changes. A set of change management operators are then introduced and form a change management language, which describes changes in a formal, declarative manner. Change enactment techniques implement the change language onto two levels: schema and instance-level.

This book covers an impressive number of topics with great clarity and presents a wealth of research ideas and techniques that will excite any researcher or practitioner wishing to understand service change management. It is nice to see that diverse and complex topics relating to service change management are explained in a eloquent manner and include extensive references to help the interested reader find out more information about these topics. Long-winded explanations that are the norm with books handling complex problems are avoided, and examples are given to enhance readability and comprehension. All in all this is an impressive piece of work and an invaluable source of knowledge for advanced students and researchers working in or wishing to know about this exciting field.

I commend the authors on the breadth and depth of their work and for producing a well thought out and eminently readable book on such a difficult topic. Enjoy!

Michael P. Papazoglou

Tilburg, The Netherlands, November 2010

Preface

The rapid adoption of Web services is motivating a paradigm shift in enterprise structure from the traditional single entity to a collaboration of Web services. Such enterprises will open the door of entrepreneurship to all Web users by facilitating functionality outsourcing on the Web. Required functionality may be outsourced to third party Web-based providers through service composition. A *composed* Web service is an on-demand and dynamic collaboration between autonomous Web services that collectively provide a value added service. Each autonomous service specializes in a core competency,which reduces cost with increased quality and efficiency for the business entity and its consumers.

A Long term Composed service (LCS) has a long term business objective and commitment to its customers. It has attracted significant attentions since it empowers a business to offer value-added and customized services to its customers. To realizing LCSs, it is essential to deal with changes during their lifetime. Due to the dynamic nature of Web service infrastructure, changes should be considered as the *rule* and managed in a structured and systematic way. Changes can be classified into two categories: *top-down* and *bottom-up* changes. Top-down changes are initiated by the business entity. They are usually the result of business policies, business regulations, or laws. Bottom-up changes are initiated by the outsourced service providers. They are usually the result of an error, an exception, or an alteration in a Web service. Web services may change their features independently without the consent or knowledge of the LCS that utilizes their functionality. Once a change occurs, a LCS must react in a reasonable time and realign itself to deal with the change. This alignment must be performed in an automatic manner considering the frequent occurrence of the changes to an LCS. By doing this, the LCS can not only deal with unanticipated changes to the underlying services and infrastructure, but also maximize its market value, optimize functionality outsourcing, and maintain competitiveness.

In this book, we propose an end-to-end framework that manages both top-down and bottom-up changes. We first define semantic support that provides the necessary grounding semantics to support the automation of change management. We then propose a supporting infrastructure for a LCS, which is based on a so-called LCS schema. The LCS schema gives a high-level overview of a LCS's key features. It allows a structured and disciplined way to manage changes. For top-down changes, we propose a change management language, SCML, to specify the changes in a formal, declarative, unambiguous, and complete way. We then propose a process of change enactment which implements the change language. We also propose a process to verify the process of change enactment which ensures that the correctness of a LCS has been maintained. Considering that there may be multiple candidates for the result of change management, we propose an optimizing process to achieve the "best" result. For bottom-up changes, we propose a petri net based change model. We first propose a taxonomy of bottom-up changes, which classifies them into different categories. Based on this taxonomy, different change functions are then defined. These changes are then mapped using petri nets. Since bottom-up changes are usually disruptive and unplanned, we propose a change detection process. Detection involves a service agent that monitors the member Web service. Each change type has an associated set of rules for detection. Once a bottom-up change is detected, it will be promptly and accurately propagated through the LCS for reaction. All affected components of the LCS will be informed of the change within a reasonable time frame. Every change that is communicated to the LCS initiates a reactive process. We propose a set of reaction rules to support this process. The reaction rules specify the course of action for the LCS to manage the change.

Xumin Liu
Salman Akram
Athman Bouguettaya

Acknowledgements

I would like to thank my parents, my sisters, and my brother for their constant love and support. I want to thank my daughter, Emily, for the happiness, sunshine, and enjoyable moments she has brought to my life. My most special appreciation goes to my husband Qi Yu for his continuous encouragement, everlasting support, and deep love.

I would like to thank Zaki Malik, Xiaobing Wu, and Li Zhou for their valuable input to this book. I would also like to appreciate the support from my employer, Rochester Institute of Technology.

Xumin Liu

I would like to thank my parents for their continuous encouragement, love, and commitment to my education. I thank my sisters for their emotional support while I was working on this book. I also would like to thank my daughter, Aizah, for giving me the energy and dedication to take on this challenge. My wife, Sameera, has been a firm foundation throughout the process and I thank her for the patience and continuous motivation.

Salman Akram

I would like to acknowledge the support of my family during the preparation of this book: my wife Malika, my children: Zakaria, Ayoub, and Mohamed-Islam. I would also like to thank my employer CSIRO (Australia) for providing me the environment to successfully finish this work.

Athman Bouguettaya

Contents

Chapter 1
Introduction

The last few years have witnessed a plethora of activity around Web services [71, 84, 89, 55, 39, 27, 85, 10, 98, 87]. Web services are gradually taking root as a result of convergence of business and government efforts to make the Web the primary medium of interaction [61]. Furthermore, the maturity of XML-based Web service standards, such as *SOAP* and *WSDL*, are driving the rapid adoption of Web services [28, 17].

Web services enable large scale application integration in a distributed, heterogeneous, and dynamic environment. A Web service is defined as a software system designed to support interoperable machine-to-machine interaction over a network [9]. It is the central component in a *Web service architecture*. A Web service architecture consists of three roles: *service providers*, *service consumers*, and *service brokers* (depicted in Figure 1.1). A service provider offers business functionalities. A service consumer uses Web services. A service broker mediates between a service provider and a service consumer. It enables a service provider to publish services and a service consumer to discover services. A Web service architecture also incorporates three key XML-based standards to support the roles and their interaction. These standards include *Web Service Description Language* (WSDL), *Simple Object Access Protocol* (SOAP), and *Universal Description Discovery and Integration* (UDDI). WSDL defines a Web service as a set of endpoints operating on messages [92]. It is used by a service provider to publish their services. SOAP defines a communication protocol that can be used by a service consumer to access Web services [90]. UDDI defines a registry for advertising and discovering Web services [91].

The rapid adoption of Web services is motivating a paradigm shift in enterprise structure from the traditional single entity to a collaboration of Web services. Such enterprises will open the door of entrepreneurship to all Web users by facilitating functionality outsourcing on the Web. Required functionality may be outsourced to third party Web-based providers through service composition [5]. A *composed* Web service is an on-demand and dynamic collaboration between autonomous Web services that collectively provide a

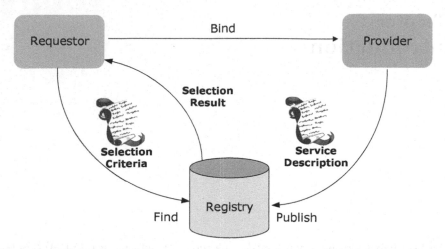

Fig. 1.1   Web Service Model

value added service. Each autonomous service specializes in a core competency, which reduces cost with increased quality and efficiency for the business
entity and its consumers.

There are two types of composed Web services: *short term* and *long term.*
In a short term composed service, both the business objective and Web service
partnerships are temporary and short lived. Once the business objective is
achieved, the partnerships between Web services are dissolved. An example
of such short term composed Web services is a trip planer, which may be
invoked by a user to plan a family summer vacation. This planner may be
a collaboration between various travel services, such as airlines, hotels, and
car rentals. Once the travel planning is complete, the trip planner will no
longer be needed by the user and the collaboration between the Web services
must be dissolved. In a *Long term Composed Service* (LCS), the business
objective of the composed service spans across multiple transactions and
over a long period of time. Partnerships between services may or may not
be long term. The services are composed to fulfill a business goal in the
long run. A typical application of a LCS is a *Service Oriented Enterprise*
(SOE) [57], which has a long term business objective and commitment to
its users. Long term composed services (LCSs) have attracted significant
attention since they empower a business to offer value-added and customized
services to its customers. While there has been a large body of research in the
automatic composition of Web services, managing changes during the LCS
lifecycle has so far attracted little attention [5, 101, 18].

1.1 Motivation

A LCS consists of several autonomous outsourced Web services, but acts as a *virtually* coherent entity. Business entities, in the form of Web services, are often geographically distributed and organizationally independent. While LCSs have a potential to introduce new business opportunities through dynamic alliances, the challenges of fully realizing a LCS lie in managing changes during its lifecycle.

1.1.1 Long term Composed Services

LCSs aim at leveraging existing online services by forming dynamic alliances to provide value-added services. As more and more business entities offer functionality and services on the Web via Web services, LCSs have become the new paradigm that enables flexible and on-demand collaboration between different business entities. Application domains of LCSs include scientific computing, tourism industry, computer industry, automobile industry, etc. We summarize several benefits of LCSs below.

- *Cost:* The provisioning of Web services drastically reduces the time and capital required to start a business. Web services are readily available for integration and orchestration, and therefore reduce the time to market for an enterprise. Furthermore, investments made by other businesses may be reused for mutual profit and a reduced start up cost for the LCS.
- *Dynamism:* The partners of LCSs can be selected dynamically. Web services provide machine-processable APIs that enable themselves to be invoked and orchestrated automatically [44]. Hence, LCSs enable an on-demand, project-driven alliance between different business entities. Moreover, there is no geographical boundary that restricts the selection of business partners. Hence, LCSs enable a wide-integration of business entities from the "global village". Finally, a Web service's market competitiveness and reputation will provide an added benefit to the LCSs.
- *Quality:* As more and more business entities have exposed their functionality as Web services, it will be possible that multiple service providers compete to offer the similar services with different user-centric quality [99]. The "best" services can be selected from those providers to form LCSs. Therefore, the consumer or end user of LCSs will benefit from the open competition between businesses.

1.1.2 Change Management

The lifecycle of a LCS is a series of stages through which it passes from its inception to its termination. There are four phases in a LCS lifecycle: *planning, composition, orchestration,* and *dissolution.* The planning phase is the first stage, where the LCS is described at a high level. It is initiated when the owner of the LCS establishes a need for a business objective [73]. The composition phase deals with integrating the selected Web services [63]. The composed Web service is then orchestrated to provide a value-added service. The dissolution phase occurs when the owner of the LCS determines that the LCS is no longer needed.

To materialize the concept of LCS, the LCS must automatically adapt to its dynamic environment, i.e., to deal with changes during its lifetime. Because of the dynamic nature of Web service infrastructure, changes should be considered as the *rule* and managed in a structured and systematic way [52]. Changes may be introduced by the occurrence of new market interests, new business regulation, or underlying service availability. Such changes require a corresponding modification of the LCS structure with respect to the functionality it provides, the performance it delivers, and the composed partner services. Once a change occurs, a LCS must react in a reasonable time and realign itself to deal with the change. This alignment must be performed in an automatic manner considering the frequent occurrence of the changes to an LCS. By doing this, the LCS can not only deal with unanticipated changes to the underlying services and infrastructure, but also maximize its market value, optimize functionality outsourcing, and maintain competitiveness.

Changes to a LCS can be categorized into two categories: *top-down changes* and *bottom-up changes.* Top-down changes are initiated by the business entity. They are usually the result of business policies, business regulations, or laws. For example, a LCS outsources its functionality from services in travel domain to offer a comprehensive travel package (referred to as a travel agency LCS). Based on a new market report, the LCS may want to expand its business by adding a new local activity service. Bottom-up changes are initiated by the outsourced service providers. They are usually the result of an error, an exception, or an alteration in a Web service. Web services may change their features independently without the consent or knowledge of the LCS that utilizes their functionality. For example, a rental car service may become unavailable because of a network failure. Alternatively, an airline reservation service provider may change the functionality of the service by adding a new operation to check flight status. In this book, we focus on dealing with both top-down and bottom-up changes.

1.1.2.1 Top Down Changes

Top-down changes to an LCS are usually voluntary, and triggered by the business environment. Changes may occur to the business policy, business regulations, or to market trends. We further categorize top down changes as:

- *Policy:* The business policy constitutes a specification of what a LCS must accomplish. It reflect a LCS's goals and business model. For example, a travel agency LCS may have the policy of "maintaining its annual income over 20 million". If the LCS fails to achieve over 20 million income annually, it needs to increase its profit by adding a new service to attract more business opportunities or deleting a service to decrease the expenses. Meanwhile, business policies change with the business environment, which may also trigger top down changes. For example, if customers consider privacy protection when choosing a travel agency, the LCS may adopt a new policy stating that all the outsourced service providers should provide privacy protection. To enforce this policy, the services that provide poor privacy protection will be replaced by services that provide better privacy protection.
- *Regulation:* The business regulations or laws may also trigger top-down changes. For example, if there is a new regulation that the online payment should be performed by a third party service, it will subsequently initiate the process of adding an online payment service to the LCS, such as VeriSign, Paypal, Amazon, or Google Checkout.
- *Voluntary:* The business may undergo changes that do not relate to policy or regulations. The changes are voluntarily initiated by the LCS owner to increase profitability, add or remove offerings, align business with personal interests, or benefit from a new market opportunity. For example, the owner of a travel agency LCS may add a cruise Web service in anticipation of a higher demand during the summer.

Changes to a LCS enforce a new *functional* or *non-functional* requirement. A functional requirement is enforced on *what* a LCS offers. For example, a travel agency LCS may be required to add a live traffic update service to attract more customers. A non-functional requirement is enforced on *how well* a LCS performs. For example, a travel agency LCS may be required to respond to its user request in a shorter time span.

1.1.2.2 Bottom Up Changes

Bottom-up changes to LCS emerge from the Web services and the underlying middleware [88, 3]. These changes occur because of the uncertainty in the Web service environment. Unlike the top-down changes that focus on the business aspects of the enterprise, bottom-up changes relate to the Web services that compose the LCS. Bottom-up changes are also usually more disruptive than top-down changes. We categorize bottom-up changes into:

- *Infrastructure:* A change in the availability of a Web service causes a disruption to the entire enterprise. For example, if the payment processing service of an LCS becomes unavailable, it may cause the entire LCS to disrupt services.
- *Description:* Web services description provides critical information such as binding and URLs to the service consumer. Therefore, any changes to the Web service description will be disruptive for the LCS. For example, a Web service provider may decide to change the hosting provider for the service. In this case, the Web service description will be updated accordingly. Failure to manage this change will result in loss of communication between the LCS and the partner Web service.
- *Offering:* A Web service provider may decide to add, remove, or change the types of services it provides. For example, a credit card processor may add the functionality to process American Express credit cards in addition to the existing cards. This, in turn, will enable the LCS to offer the service to its users.

1.2 A Travel Scenario

In this Section, we use the travel domain as a running example to motivate and illustrate our work. Consider a travel agency LCS that aims to provide a comprehensive travel package that outsources the functionality from various service providers, such as airline, hotel, taxi, weather, and online payment (depicted in Figure 1.2). Customers are able to book airline tickets, reserve hotel rooms, reserve limos, or check weather information by directly accessing this LCS. Currently, users can directly invoke the independent services by providing the required information. When these services are combined together as an LCS, the LCS will invoke the services on behalf of the user. There may potentially be some dependency relationship between them. These dependencies determine the composition of the services. In the case of the travel agency LCS, users do not necessarily need to provide the information for each service. The input of some services can be derived from the dependency relationship. For example, when invoking an airline service and a hotel service at the same time (i.e., they are included in the same travel agency LCS), the input information for the hotel service is determined by the flight information, which is the output of the flight service. Specifically, the city and the check in and check out dates of the hotel service are all determined by the flight information. These dependency relationships need to be enforced when composing Web services together.

LCS's dynamic business environment will trigger changes to the LCSs. Suppose that a market survey shows that car rental services have attracted

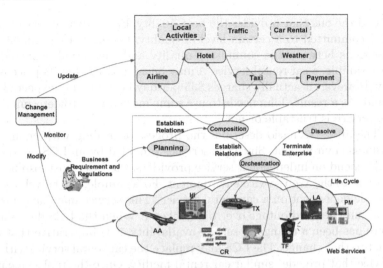

Fig. 1.2 Change reaction for adding a car rental service

more interest than taxi services serving as the ground transportation. In this case, the owner of the travel agency LCS may want to replace the taxi service by a car rental service. Moreover, users that choose car rental services are probably interested in driving direction from the airport to the hotel. Driving information may change for some reason (such as road construction). Therefore, the traffic service outsourced is expected to provide the up-to-date traffic information. In addition, there may be a growing demand to include local activities within the travel packages. For example, when a user plans a trip to Orlando, s/he may also want to visit Universal Studios and Sea World. In this case, s/he may want to reserve the tickets for these activities via the travel agency LCS. If the travel agency LCS does not incorporate local activities Web service into the enterprise, it risks becoming obsolete and loosing business.

To implement the changes mentioned above, the travel agency LCS needs to add three types of services including: car rental, traffic, and local activities. It must also remove the taxi service. Once there is an update on the participation of services in a LCS, the service composition needs to be re-generated. Therefore, the owner of the LCS, say John, needs to first examine the specification of each type of participating services. He then needs to design the composition between these services, including their data mappings and invocation order. He then needs to locate partner Web services that provide the desired functionality. Moreover, when adding a service, there may be multiple service providers that compete with each other to provide similar functionality. These service providers are different from each other in terms of their delivered quality, such as the cost and response time. In this case, John needs to find the one that provides the best quality. Each of these service providers have committed to a certain level of quality. However, there might be some violations between the committed quality and the actual delivered quality. For example, a car rental service A may be advertised that its price is $30 per day. However, it actually charges $35 per day because of unexpected high demand. As a result, John needs to use some mechanisms to determine whether the service is trustable or not.

The above scenario describes the process of dealing with changes to the business environment. Since the services provided by an LCS are outsourced and depend on independent service providers, the LCS must also be aware of changes to the Web service environment. For example, the travel agency LCS may be dependent on a car rental service. This service may have a scheduled or an unscheduled outage over the weekend. When the LCS determines that there has been a change in service availability, it is imperative that the LCS react to that change. The LCS may replace the car rental service with another service that provides similar car rental facility. Once the replacement service is discovered, the service composition needs to be re-generated. Similar to business environment changes, John needs to first examine the specification of the replacement service and then redesign the composition between these services.

This scenario justifies that the process of change management can be very complicated and time intensive, which makes it impractical to manage changes manually. Therefore, a systematic framework is required to provide automated support for change management in LCSs.

1.3 Research Issues

Managing changes to LCSs poses a set of research issues. A LCS outsources its functionality from independent service providers. There are no central control mechanisms that can be used to monitor and manage these service providers. Therefore, the challenge of managing changes lies in providing an end-to-end framework to specify and manage top down and bottom up changes. We summarize the major research issues of managing changes in LCSs as follows:

R1:   **Semantics support:** To enable the automation of change management, it is essential that software system can "understand" or intelligently parse the issues they are dealing with and the resolution approaches they can utilize. Specifically, they need to have sufficient knowledge about LCSs and their outsourced services. In databases, the automation of data queries and updates relies on metadata (i.e., data types and data schema). Similar *meta-information* is also required to provide a semantic support for the process of change management.

R2: **Change Specification:** Formally specifying changes is a prerequisite to managing changes. It is important to identify strategies for handling various types of changes. Top-down changes are initiated by a LCS's owner to cater for new business requirements, business regulations, or laws. The LCS owner is aware of the changes before implementing them. Therefore, the purpose of modeling top-down changes is to provide a methodology to specify the changes in a systematic and formal way so as to the specification can be translated to a set of change enactment algorithms. Bottom-up changes, on the other hand, are initiated by outsourced service providers. These changes usually occur without the consent to the LCS. They need to be detected first and then be handled. Therefore, the purpose of modeling bottom-up changes is to use the change models as the reference models for the detection and subsequent management of changes.

R3: **Change Management:** For top-down changes, change management consists of change enactment, change verification, and change optimization. Change enactment is to implement a specified change. A top-down change is always associated with a new requirement. It may require the LCS to add a new functionality to comply with a new requirement on the LCS. Therefore, the implementation of a change is the procedure that modifies a LCS, such as change the services that it outsources or the way that the outsourced services interact with each other. Change verification refers to the procedure that verifies the correctness of a LCS configuration. Once a top-down change has been enactment, the LCS may be reconfigured. Any reconfiguration to a LCS needs to be verified to ensure that the LCS evolves from one *correct* state to another *correct* state. For example, in a travel agency LCS, the hotel service may rely on an airline service to provide the customers' check in and check out information. Suppose that a change requires to remove the airline service. If the hotel service can not get the information from the user or other services in the LCS, its orchestration will fail. Verification must be based on a well-defined *correctness* of LCSs. Change optimization refers to the procedure that optimize the result of change management. Considering the large amount of Web services available on the Web, there may be multiple services that compete to provide similar functionalities with different performance. For example, there are multiple service providers that offer airline services, such as United, Delta, and Continental. Therefore, when a change requires a replacement of a Web service, multiple candidates may be available. This triggers a need to choose the "best" Web service from the pool of available candidates. For bottom-up changes, change management consists of change detection, change propagation, and change reaction. Change detection is to detect the behavior of the change so that the appropriate reacting policy can be chosen for the subsequent change management procedure. Change propagation is to notify the event to the LCS owner and other component services. Change reaction is to implement a reaction policy to ensure there is no disruption to LCS services.

1.4 Summary of Contributions

In this book, we propose a comprehensive, end-to-end framework that addresses the above research issues. The framework uses different strategies to deal with different types of changes. We summarize our contribution as follows.

We first define semantic support that provides the necessary grounding semantics to support the automation of change management. The semantic support is based on a hierarchical Web service ontology. The Web service ontology leverages the advantages of current semantic Web service technologies and addresses their limitations. It defines a meaningful organization of Web services as well as captures their key features. The semantics defined in the Web service ontology facilitates automatic service discovery and composition. We also propose a set of algorithms to efficiently retrieve required semantics from a Web service ontology.

We propose a supporting infrastructure for a LCS, which is based on the *LCS schema*. The LCS schema gives a high-level description of a LCS. The LCS schema captures what a LCS offers and how it works. It plays a similar role in a LCS as a database schema plays for a database. The design of the supporting infrastructure enables a clear differentiation between a high-level workflow of a LCS and low-level interactive details of the component services. Therefore, it allows a structured and disciplined way to handle a change once it occurs. We also define a set of rules to determine the correctness of a LCS's configuration. The rules can be used as the guidance of change verification.

We propose a change management language, SCML, to specify top-down changes in LCSs. We first propose a taxonomy of changes, which classifies top-down changes into different categories. Based on this taxonomy, various change operators are then defined. These operators constitute a change management language, which describes a change in a *formal* and *declarative* way. We then propose a process of change enactment which implements the change language on two levels: *schema-level* and *instance-level*. During the first level of change reaction, a LCS schema will be modified to conform to the change requirement. There are two major types of modifications at this level. First, a LCS may change the list of outsourced services. For example, it may find a new service to outsource or terminate its partnership with an outsourced service. Second, a LCS may change the way that it outsources services. For example, it may want to serialize the invocation order between two services, instead of parallelizing it. During the second level of change reaction, a new instantiation of a LCS schema will be generated. Web services that fulfill the change requirement will be selected and orchestrated. Considering that there may be multiple service providers competing to offer the similar functionality, multiple instances of the LCS can be generated.

We propose a process to verify the change reaction and ensure that the change has been managed correctly. We propose a set of verification algorithms, which are based on the defined correctness criteria. Once there is a modification made on a LCS schema, the modification will be verified. If an error is detected, it will be rectified by further modifying the LCS. We propose a two-phase process to optimize the result of change management. Web services are provided by independent service providers, which makes it very difficult to determine the level of quality initially [63, 70]. Web services may at times fail to deliver on the committed quality. Therefore, during the first phase of optimization, we use a *service reputation* as a filter to remove the Web services that have a low reputation. During the second phase, we use *Quality of Web Services* (QoWS) to define a cost model, which represents the users' preference on their choices of Web services. We then use this cost model as the second filter to choose the best one from the remaining trustworthy services.

We propose a petri net based change model to specify bottom-up changes. We first propose a taxonomy of bottom-up changes, which classifies them into different categories. Based on this taxonomy, different change functions are then defined. These changes are then mapped using petri nets. Since bottom-up changes are usually disruptive and unplanned, we propose a change detection process. Detection involves a service agent that monitors the member Web service. Each change type has an associated set of rules for detection. Once a bottom-up change is detected, it will be promptly and accurately propagated through the LCS for reaction. All affected components of the LCS will be informed of the change within a reasonable time frame. Every change that is communicated to the LCS initiates a reactive process. We propose a set of reaction rules to support this process. The reaction rules specify the course of action for the LCS to manage the change.

1.5 Literature Review

Change management is an active research area. Although it is relative new in the Web service community, some frameworks have been proposed for managing changes for process-oriented systems, such as workflows [34, 16, 78, 53, 83, 66]. In this chapter, we overview some related work in this area.

1.5.1 Change Management in Web Service Community

In [12], a framework is presented to detect and react to the exceptional changes that can be raised inside workflow-driven Web application is proposed. It first classifies these changes into *behavioral (or user-generated)*, *semantic (or application)*, and *system* exceptions. The behavior exceptions are driven by improper execution order of process activities. For example, the free user navigation through Web pages may result in the wrong invocation of the expired link, or double-click the link when only one click is respected. The semantic exceptions are driven by unsuccessful logical outcome of activities execution. For example, a user does not keep paying his periodic installments. The system exceptions are driven by the malfunctioning of the workflow-based Web application, such as network failures and system break-downs. It then proposes a modeling framework that describes the structure of activities inside hypertext of a Web application. The hypertext belonging to an activity is broken down into pages, where are identified within an activity. framework to handle these changes. The framework consists of three major components: *capturing model, notifying model,* and *handling model.* The capturing model capture events and store the exceptions data in the workflow model. The notifying model propagate the occurred exceptions to the users. The handling model defines a set of recovery policy to resolve the exception. For different types of exceptions, different recovery policies will be used.

In [76], a framework is presented to manage the business protocol evolution in service-oriented architecture. It uses several features to handling the running instances under the old protocol. These features include *impact analysis* and *data mining based migration analysis.* The impact analysis is to analyze how protocol change impacts on the running instances. It will be used to determine whether ongoing conversations are *migrateable* to the new protocol or not. The data mining based migration analysis is used for cases where the regular impact analysis cannot be performed. Service interaction logs are analyzed using data mining techniques. It then uses the result of the analysis to determine whether a conversion is *migrateable* or not. In [76], the work mainly deals with dynamic protocol evolution. We focus on automatically modifying the composition of Web services once there is a new requirement introduced by a change.

1.5.2 Adaptive Workflow System

Workflows are the popular means of composing enterprises. They provide the ability to execute business processes that span multiple organizations [79]. Traditional workflows do not provide methods for dynamic change management. Workflows are geared towards *static* integration of components. This characteristic inhibits the profitability, adaptability, utility, and creativity in an enterprise. Furthermore, workflows do not cater for the behavioral aspects of Web services. For example, they do not distinguish between the internal and external processes of a Web service [15].

Workflow management systems (*WfMS*) aim at coordinating activities between different business processes (systems) so they can run in an efficient manner. This is done by automating the business processes and invoking appropriate resources in a sequence. According to the WfMC [24], "workflow is concerned with the automation of procedures where documents, information or tasks are passed between participants according to a defined set of rules to achieve or contribute to an overall business goal."

[34] focuses on modeling dynamic changes within workflow system. It first identifies a set of modalities of changes, including change duration, change lifetime, change medium, change time-frame, change continuity, change agents, change rules, and change migration. The change duration specifies whether the change is to happen quickly (instantaneous) or over a noticeable long (but finite and well specified) time period or an unspecified amount of time (indefinite). The change lifetime specifies the amount of time that the change is in effect. The change medium specifies the medium to make change, such as human (manually), software agents (automatic), or mixture. The change time-frame specifies whether the change should enforce constraints on the work-cases that are currently in progress. The change continuity specifies the migration strategy, such as preemptive or integrative. The change agents specifies which participants play which organizational roles within the change process. The change rules guide a change process in its pursuit of meeting the goals that changes come to life to achieve. Change migration refers to the ability to bring the filtered-in cases into compliance with the new procedure in accordance with the migration policies agreed upon by the change designers. This work then introduces a Modeling Language to support Dynamic Evolution within Workflow System (ML-DEWS). A change is modeled as a process class, which contains the information of *roll-out time*, *expiration time*, *change filter*, and *migration process*. The roll-out time indicates when the change begins. The expiration time indicates when the change ends. The change filter specifies the old cases that are allowed to migrate to the new procedure. The migration process specifies how the filtered-in old cases migrate to the new process.

[75] presents a Petri net based approach to maintaining correctness between process *type* and *instances*. A process type represents a particular business process described by a schema. Process instance is a real time execution of the process type. Changes to process type occur when the process schema is modified in response to the environment. For example, a business process may adapt to comply with new legislation, or it may be optimized for performance reasons. The respective process type changes must be propagated to the process instances. Inversely, process instances may be changed to accommodate for changes in the execution environment. For example, an exception may cause the process to skip a task. A mapping of this instance to the process type results in a schema that is different from the original process schema. When process type and instance changes are executed independently, they are no longer in harmony with each other.

1.5.3 Change Management in Traditional Databases

Several change detection algorithms have been proposed to measure changes in Web content and also XML documents [19, 25]. Most of the algorithms that deal with changes in Web content aim to maintain the consistency of data on the Web site. They do provide mechanisms to "understand" what the data represents and react appropriately. Research on detecting changes to XML documents has been mainly focused on the syntactic changes to a document. For example, [25] provides an efficient algorithm that detects *structural* change to an XML document. It does not efficiently detect *semantic* changes to XML documents such as WSDL descriptions. Furthermore, [25] deals with detecting changes after a *move* operation.

Similarly, [19] proposes the detection of changes in hierarchical data. This data is primarily nested and is not represented by a unique identifier. It proposes techniques for comparison between two structured data versions. However, these techniques do not deal with the Web service environment. Therefore, change detection is only at the abstract layer and cannot be readily applied to Web services.

1.5.4 Ontologies for Web Services

There are two major purposes to markup semantic Web service description. First, adding semantics to service description is to enable automatic service composition. It means that software agents can automatically select, compose, and interoperate Web services given a high-level description of a requirement. To reach this goal, a service description needs to provide declarative specification of the IOPE (Input, Output, Precondition, Effect) of the service. Second, adding semantics to service description is to facilitate efficient access to Web services. It means that software agents can optimize an execution plan from the multiple competitive services for a given requirement. To reach this goal, service description must provide declarative specification of the quality of Web services. A research trend for semantically describing Web services is to build ontologies for Web services.

The term *ontology* originates from philosophy. In that context, an ontology is used to describe existing objects by grouping them into abstract classes based on shared properties. Since the beginning of the 1990s, ontologies have been used in artificial intelligence areas to facilitate knowledge sharing and reuse. In a nutshell, ontologies improve communications among humans and software entities by providing "*the common understanding of a domain of interest* [4]." Many definitions of ontologies have been offered. The most cited one, which best characterizes the essence of an ontology, is "*an explicit and formal specification of a conceptualization* [42]." *Conceptualization* refers to an abstract model that encapsulates the properties of objects and activities of the real world. An ontology should describe knowledge in a way that is same as what people take to conceive the world. *Formal specification* refers to the fact that knowledge should be specified in a machine-processible language. *Explicit specification* refers to the fact that concepts and their relationships should be defined explicitly. An ontology should avoid of containing implicit information to decrease confusion in knowledge specification. An ontology contains a vocabulary of terms (e.g. people, stuff, courses) in a given domain. These terms can be presented in an ontology in form of classes (concepts). The relationships between these terms can be shaped as a lattice or taxonomy of classes and subclasses. Ontologies are different in their degrees of formality. At one end, ontologies like Dublin Core [95] and WordNet [36] provide a thesaurus for large number of terms to explain online information. At other end of the spectrum, ontologies like CYC [56] and KIF [38] provide formal axiomating theories based on the first-order predicate calculus. A tradeoff exists between the two contributions of an ontology: knowledge expressiveness and reasoning supports.

OWL

DAML+OIL was adopted by W3C as a starting point of OWL, an ontology language for the Semantic Web [94]. OWL builds on the syntax of RDF and RDF Schema. Moreover, it tackles the expressive limitations of RDF. RDF defines the online resources and their relationships by modeling them as classes. It also describe their relationships. However, it fails to provide the other important features for reasoning. For example, if x is a subclass of y and y is a subclass of z, we can know that x is a subclass of z. However, RDF cannot express such transitive property of subclass relationships. OWL adopts the RDF meaning of classes and properties and add more language primitives for online resource inference. These primitives define transitive, symmetric, and inverse properties of classes. They also define boolean combinations (union, intersection, and complement) to support flexibly reasoning online resources.

OWL-S

As a key evolution of distributed applications, Web services are experiencing a fast growth. Ontologies help enrich the semantic descriptions of Web services to facilitate automation of service discovery, service invocation, service composition, service interoperation, and service execution monitoring. OWL-S [29] is a representative ontology language built on OWL for Web services. It provides a set of markup language constructs for describing properties and functionalities of Web services in a machine-understandable manner.

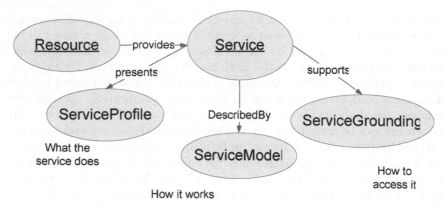

Fig. 1.3 The OWL-S for Web Services

As showed in Figure 1.3, OWL-S describes a Web service from four aspects, including service provider, service capabilities, service execution process, and service accesses. These four aspects are respectively represented by four classes, including **resource**, **serviceProfile**, **serviceModel**, and **serviceGrounding**. The serviceProfile provides a high-level view on Web services. It describes information about a service function, including the service provider, functional description, and the service characteristics. The functional description specifies the required input and the generated output of the service. It also specifies the preconditions and effects. The serviceProfile plays the similar roles on Web service representation as what UDDI plays. The difference between the capabilities of serviceProfile and UDDI is that serviceProfile enriches more semantics. The serviceProfile also supports automatic Web service discovery. The serviceModel provides a detailed view on how a service operates as a process. A process consists of a set of tasks and their execution order. The specified information of a process includes its input, output, preconditions, and effects. The input/output relates to the processes that transform data. The precondition/effect relates to the processes that change the state of the world. The serviceModel also specifies data flows and parameter bindings. It enables agents to derive the services choreography. It thus supports automatic Web service composition. The serviceGrounding specifies the detail of how to access Web services. It mainly describes the binding information of services, including protocols, message formats, serialization, transport, and addressing. It thus can be used to support automatic Web service invocations.

WSMO

Web Service Modeling Ontology (WSMO) is an ontology for describing several aspects of semantic Web services. It takes Web Service Modeling Framework (WSMF) [37] as a starting point. The WSMF consists of four main parts, including *goals*, *ontologies*, *mediators*, and *Web services*. The *goal* defines the problems that a Web service is expected to address. The *ontology* defines the formal semantics for the terms used in other elements of the WSMF. The *mediator* is used to address interoperability problems, such as data mismatches and process sequence mismatches. The *Web service* part defines several elements to describe a Web service, including the precondition, post-condition, data flow, control flow.

WSMO refines the WSMF and defines these elements in a formal fashion. The WSMO definition of a Web service consists of four parts, including *nonFunctionalProperties*, *usedMediators*, *capability*, and *interface*. The `nonFunctionalProperties` describe the properties that are not directly related to a Web service's functionality, such as service providers, cost, performance, reliability, and security. These properties are mainly used to help software agents discover and select Web services. They can also be used for negotiation. The `usedMediators` define the mediators used by a Web service. For example, a Web service can use the concepts and relationships elsewhere by importing ontologies through ontology mediators (`ooMediators`). It can also use `wgMediator` to address interoperability problems between a Web service and goals. The `capability` defines the functionalities of a Web service. It helps software agents locate a desirable Web service. A capability can be modeled by using preconditions, postconditions, and effects. The `interface` describes how a Web service functionalities can be fulfilled. It can be used to help software agents invoke and combine Web services. The WSMO definition describes the interface of a Web service from a twofold view, including *choreography* (from user's prospective) and *orchestration* (form other service provider's perspective). The choreography describes the information about how to interact with a service to make use of its functionalities, such as Message Exchange Pattern (MEP). The orchestration describes the information about how a Web service is outsourced to provide a value-added service. It has a tight relationship with the Problem Solving Pattern (PSP), which specifies a sequence of activities to achieve a given requirement. *Web Service Modeling Language* (WSML) [96] provides a formal syntax and semantic for WSMO. It is based on well-known logical formalisms, including first-order logic, description logic, and logic programming.

1.6 Book Organization

This book is organized as follows. In Chapter 2, we propose a semantic support that offers formal semantic for automating the process of change management. The semantic support centers around a Web service ontology and a set of algorithms for retrieving semantics from the ontology. In Chapter 3, we propose a supporting infrastructure of LCSs. We describe the architecture of a LCS and define a LCS schema, which captures a LCS's feature in high-level. We also defines a set of criteria for evaluating whether a LCS schema is in a correct configuration. The criteria are used for the purpose of change verification. In Chapter 4, we propose a formal model for top-down changes. We first classify top-down changes and defined change operators for different types of changes. We then define a SQL-like language, Web Service Change Management Language (SCML), to specify top-down changes. In Chapter 5, we propose a set of algorithms to enact top-down changes. We propose a process to implement the change operators, verify the changes to ensure the correctness of a LCS, and a two-phase optimization approach to achieve the best result of change management. In Chapter 6, we propose a formal model for bottom-up changes. The model is based on a taxonomy of changes which classified different changes into different categories. This enables applying different management rules for different types of changes. In Chapter 7, we propose a process of managing bottom-up changes, including change detection, change propagation, and change reaction. In Chapter 8, we overview the related work. The book concludes with Chapter 9 by summarizing the major contributions and discussing some future directions.

Chapter 2
Semantic Support for Change Management

Semantic support is always considered as the key enabler for automation. With the help of machine-processible semantics, software agents can understand the functionality and performance of a Web service. They can then determine whether a service should be selected as a component of a LCS and how to integrate the service with other components.

Semantic Web service technologies have been proposed to automate the usage of Web services, such as service discovery and service composition. The existing approaches can be classified into two categories. The first type of approaches adds semantic markup information to a service's WSDL description [93, 23, 96]. The input, output, and operations of a Web service are annotated with machine-understandable information. Such semantic annotations can help software agent software agents discover and invoke a Web service. The limitation of this type of approaches is that they mainly focus on the semantics within a service description. They do not capture the inter-service relationship, which can be used to facilitate in locating Web services in a large scale and composing different services together. The second type of approaches builds up a meaningful organization of Web services. The services having the same functionality are grouped into the same categories, *a.k.a., service communities* [62]. When a service provider registers the service to a service registry, such as UDDI, it will publish the service description, together with the information about its associated service community. The limitation of this type of approaches is that they lack sufficient semantic description for Web services. Moreover, service communities are *flat*. Querying a service community is always keyword-based and not optimized. In additional to their limitations, different approaches have different assumptions and focuses. This also makes them not suitable enough for supporting automatic change reaction.

In this chapter, we propose a semantic support that are expected to play a key role in automating the process of change management. The central of the semantic support is a Web service ontology that has a hierarchical structure, which leverages the advantages of current approaches and addresses their limitations.

2.1 A Tree-Structured Web Service Ontology

In this section, we propose a *Web service ontology* that provides enough semantics for the schema modifier and service selector. As depicted in Figure 2.1, the ontology has a tree-like structure. Each node in the tree represents a *service concepts*. It also captures the relationship between different nodes, which can be leveraged for efficiently locating and composing Web services.

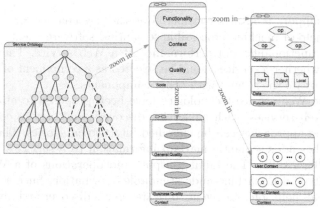

Fig. 2.1   A Web service ontology

2.1.1 Service Concepts

A service concept defines a type of Web services within a domain. It can be considered as a service category, which groups Web services based on their functionality. Using the service concepts of the ontology, Web services' functionalities are defined in a way that is clear and unambiguous to software agents. For example, classifying a Web service instance *w* to the "AirBooking" node of the ontology implies that it is an air reservation service. This ontology also facilitates a LCS's owner to establish its LCS. The owner can choose a node of this ontology as an abstract service to define the LCS schema.

A Web service has three major properties: *service functionality* ($\mathcal{F}^S$), *service context* ($\mathcal{C}^S$), and *service quality* ($\mathcal{Q}^S$). $\mathcal{F}^S$ specifies what a service offers to its users. $\mathcal{C}^S$ constructs the environmental situation that a service operates with. $\mathcal{Q}^S$ defines a set of parameters for service evaluation and selection. By using the information delivered by these three features, a LCS can determine whether to choose a service as its member (i.e. whether the service provides the desirable functionality with satisfactory context and quality). These three features are elaborated on in the following sections.

2.1.1.1 Functionality

A service functionality ($\mathcal{F}^S$) is collectively delivered by a set of *service operations*. The process of accessing a service is actually invoking one or more operations provided by the service. The operations consume the service input and generate the output of the service.

It is worthy to note that there may be dependency relationships between different service operations. For example, an Airline service may provide several operations, such as `user_login` and `flight_reservation`. Typically, an user needs to login before (s)he can reserve an air ticket. Therefore, there is a dependency between `user_login` and `flight_reservation`. The dependencies between service operations (referred to as *operation-level dependencies*) need to be strictly enforced when accessing a service.

A service data is also an essential aspect of a service functionality. A service is actually affected by the outside with a set of input and responses with a set of output [2].

Therefore, we can define a service functionality as a binary: service data (D) and service operations (OP). D is an essential aspect of the behavior of a service. A service can be viewed as a transducer that translates a set of input items into a set of output items [2]. Besides of these input (I), output (O) data, D also contains internal data (N), which the service generates and consumes them by itself. OP consists of a set of operations and their dependency relationships.

There are several ontology languages such as OWL-S and WSMO [23, 96] that we can use to describe the proposed ontology. Take OWL-S as an example. There is a mapping between the proposed service ontology and the OWL-S definition. A service data can be mapped to the property of hasInput, hasOuput, hasLocal. A service operation can be mapped to the definition of an atomic process. The relationship between two operations can be defined by a composite process in an OWL-S ontology.

Suppose that an airline service provides a flight ticket reservation functionality. It has the service data as follows:

(I)={user_information, departure_date, arrival_date, departure_city, arrival_city}.
(O)={flight_information}
(N)={login_confirmation, payment_information}
The airline service also has the service operations as follows:

user_Login: It takes user_information as input and generates the output of login_information and payment_information.

flight_Reservation: It takes the input of login_confirmation, payment_information, departure_date, arrival_date, departure_city, arrival_city and generates the output of flight_inforamation.

It can be specified in OWL-S as depicted in Figure 2.2.

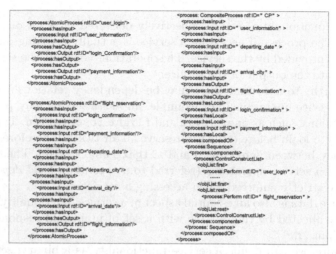

Fig. 2.2 An example of an airline service ontology in OWL-S

2.1.1.2 Quality

The service quality (Q^S) is the main criterion to evaluate a service [26, 65, 69, 47]. A Web service is always associated with a service in the real world (e.g. an airline company or a hotel). Therefore, we define the service quality in twofold: *general quality* (Q_G) and *business quality* (Q_B).

- General quality consists of a set of domain-free parameters that measure the quality of the service that is consumed through the Web. It mainly presents the measurement of properties that are related to the access of an operation *op* of a Web service. Examples of these parameters include *availability*, *reliability*, and *latency*. The general quality also includes the security requirements that are compliant with an operation *op* of a Web service. Examples of the parameters include *encryption*, *authentication*, and *reputation*.

- Business quality consists of a set of domain-specific parameters that measure the quality of the service that is consumed in the real world. For

example, in a travel domain, the parameters can be the *fee* that is charged
to access a service, *comfort_Lodge* for how comfort is a lodge service, and
convenience_Internet for how convenient the access to the Internet.

Table 2.1 Measurement of QoWS parameters

Category	Parameter	Definition	Domain
General	Latency	$Time_{process}(op)$ + $Time_{results}(op)$ where $Time_{process}$ is the time to process op and $Time_{results}$ is the time to transmit/receive the results	number
	Reliability	$N_{success}(op)/N_{invoked}(op)$ where $N_{success}$ is the number of times that op has been successfully executed and $N_{invoked}$ is the total number of invocations	number
	Availability	UpTime(op)/TotalTime(op) where UpTime is the time op was accessible during the total measurement time TotalTime	number
	Encryption	Equal to 1 iff messages are encrypted	number
	Authentication	Equal to 1 iff consumers are authenticated	number
	Reputation	The degree of confidence that a service will deliver the quality it promises, ranging from 0 to 1.	number
Business (travel domain)	Fee	Dollar amount to execute the operation	number
	comfort_Lodge	The degree of comfort provided by a lodge service, ranging from 0 to 1	number
	convenience_Internet	The degree of convenience of accessing Internet, ranging from 0 to 1	number

We propose a QoWS model as depicted in Table 2.1. It is not meant to
be exhaustive and can be extended. It gives the formal definitions of a set of
representative quality parameters. Other quality parameters can be added to
extend the current model.

2.1.1.3 Context

The context of a Web service ($\mathcal{C}^{\mathcal{S}}$) models the environmental situation that
a service resides in. It can be any metadata that explicitly describes the
meaning of the data items exchanged between Web services. For example,
context=(currency, dollars) defines a context of currency in dollars. Therefore, $\mathcal{C}^{\mathcal{S}}$ contains the important information for correctly interacting with a
service and needs to be modeled in a formal way.

Since a service context can be of any type of metadata, there are many
types of contexts, such as *location, time, currency, temperature, weight, length,*
and *users*. Therefore, we define C as a set of context types that are related
to the service invocation. $C = \{c_1, ..., c_n\}$, where c_i is a context type.

```
<env:Envelope xmlns:env="http://schemas.xmlsoap.org/soap/envelope/">
    <env:Header>
        <Context xmlns="http://sg.fmi.uni-passau.de/context">
            <Location>
                <address useType="Office">
                    <addressLine keyName="Street" keyValue="60">Fairfax Rd</addressLine>
                    <addressLine keyName="City" keyValue="40">Falls church</addressLine>
                </address>
            </Location>
            <Client>
                <payment useType="Online Payment">
                    <paymentLine keyName="Type" keyValue="20">Visa</paymentLine>
                    <paymentLine keyName="IssueBy" keyValue="30">the United States</paymentLine>
                </payment>
            </Client>
        </Context>
    </env:Header>
    <env:Body>
        <!-- serialized object data -->
    </env:Body>
</env:Envelope>
```

Fig. 2.3 A context transported in a SOAP header block

WS-context is an OASIS standards to manage the lifecycle of a Web service context [67]. In WS-Context, the context lifecycle is as follows. First, to initiate an activity, a service requests a new context from the WS-Context service via a begin message and specifies a timeline for sharing the context. The begin action will then return a begin message plus a context. In this case, the interaction with the service will be associated with the context delivered in a SOAP message [90]. The context-aware service interaction will be terminated once by timing out or by explicitly instructing the context service to end. Figure 2.3 shows an example of a SOAP message that delivers a context information.

2.1.2 Service Relationships

We define two types of relationships between two nodes in the ontology tree: *inheritance* and *dependency*. The inheritance is between two service nodes if one inherits its features (e.g., service data and operations) from another one. This relationship can be used to facilitate in service discovery. Dependency is between two service nodes if one's invocation relies on another's invocation. This relationship can be used to automate service composition. We elaborate on these two types of relationships as follows.

2.1.2.1 Inheritance Relationship

In the traditional ontology system, an ontology only contains the relationship of "consumption" (i.e., is-a) between a node and its children. That is, the children inherit all the properties from the node. This feature is not perfectly in line with the ontology designed for a Web service domain, where partial consumption relationship (i.e., has-of) may exist between two nodes [31]. These two types of inheritance are described as follows.

- An *is-a* relationship is between a node and its parent if the node inherits all the properties (i.e., operations and service data) of the parent. The node also has the properties that the parent node does not have. For example, an Airline service is a child of a Transportation service. It provides the transportation service with a special feature, i.e., through a flight. Therefore, there is an *is-a* relationship between the Airline service and the Transportation service.
- A *has-of* relationship is between a node and its parent if the node partially inherits the properties from the parent. For example, a Flight Quote service is a child of an Airline service. It only provides the service of getting the quote of a flight, but not other airline-related services, such as checking flight status, reserving a flight, or electronic check in. Therefore, there is a *has-of* relationship between the Flight Quote service and the Airline service.

One of the important evaluation criteria of defining an ontology is to check whether the definition can achieve the common understanding among different parties. To achieve this goal, we allows these two types of inheritance in our proposed ontology to make it more intuitive. The inheritances are represented in different ways. We use a line to denote an is-a relationship and a dashed line to denote a has-of relationship.

2.1.2.2 Dependency Relationship

It is worth to note that although Web services are autonomous and they can be invoked independently, some dependency constraint may need to be enforced when they are combined together. For example, a user can invoke an airline service and a hotel service individually. However, if a user wants an airline+hotel package, the check-in and check-out information of the hotel service depends on the flight information, which is the output of the airline service. The dependency relationships between different types of services within a domain are usually generated by domain experts.

A dependency constraint can be specified as a triplet $\{S_1, S_2, D\}$. It means that the invocation of S_1 depends on the invocation of S_2 when they cooperate together since S_2's output will be used as the input of S_1 with respect to the data items included in D. The dependency constraint is not necessarily transitive. That is, if S_1 depends on S_2 and S_2 depends on S_3, S_1 does not necessarily depend on S_3. Suppose only S_1 and S_3 attend the cooperation, the dependency constraints $\{S_1, S_2, D_1\}$ and $\{S_2, S_3, D_2\}$ do not need to be enforced since S_2 is not involved in the cooperation. In this case, there may be no dependency relationship between S_1 and S_3.

2.2 Heuristic Query Process

Reacting to a change requires to refer back to the hierarchical structure of the corresponding service ontology, seeking for desired semantics. In this section, we propose an approach to efficiently query the service ontology.

2.2.1 Query Categories

Querying a Web service ontology is required to retrieve the desired service nodes and locate Web services that subscribe to them. Meanwhile, the dependency relationship between different types of services also needs to be retrieved for composing these services together. Therefore, there are three types of ontology queries required as below.

- *Functionality-based service query:* It is to traverse a Web service ontology to find a service node which offers a specified functionality. Since a service functionality has two facets: service operations and service data, there are two types of queries here: operation-based and data-based. This query will be used to update the list of a LCS schema's abstract services.
- *Dependency relationship query:* : It is to check the dependency relationship between two given service nodes. This query will be used to automatically modify a LCS schema.
- *Web service query:* It is to find a list of Web services that offer the functionality defined by the given service node. This query will be used to automatically locate a Web service.

Retrieving the dependency relationship is always performed after identifying the service node in a Web service ontology. Since the information is included in the definition of the service concept, the query can be easily done by looking into the definition. Retrieving the list of Web services given a service node can rely on the association between service nodes and Web services. The association is built when creating the service node and maintained after that. It is always stored in a service registry, such as UDDI registry. By looking up the association, the desired Web service list can be obtained.

2.2.2 Heuristic Query Process

The structure of ontology is hierarchical and extensible by nature. Once the ontology structure becomes large with the increment of the available service functionalities, the process of identifying a proper piece of functionality would turn out to be time consuming. It is important and beneficial for change reaction to make this process efficient and accurate.

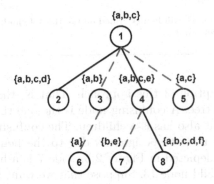

Fig. 2.4 An ontology tree

An intuitive heuristic query can be achieved by leveraging the difference between is-a and has-of relationships. That is, if a service node does not contain the required operations, its has-of children should not contain either. Therefore, only its is-a children will be further explored. For example, in the tree depicted in Figure 2.4, suppose we want to find a node providing $\{a, b, c, d, f\}$ (here, a and f refer to service operations or service data). The query starts at the root node. Since the root node does not provide d and f, the query will be further performed in the is-a children. Therefore, node 2 and node 4 will be checked. Continue the process until the desired node (i.e., node 8) is found. The process is described in Algorithm 1.

Algorithm 1 Heuristic Query on a Web Service Ontology Tree

1: **Function** HQ(r, $\mathcal{Q}$) {r is a service node, $\mathcal{Q}$ is a set of required operations or data}
2: **if** (r.$\mathcal{P}$ == $\mathcal{Q}$) **return** r; {find the match}
3: **if** (($\mathcal{Q}$-r.$\mathcal{P}$) <> $\emptyset$){the current node does not cover the required set}
4:    N = get_Is_a_Children(r);
5:    **for all** ($n \in$ N)
6:       S=HQ(n, $\mathcal{Q}$); {the search will be performed on the is-a children}
7:       **if** (S <>NULL) **return** S;
8:    **return** NULL;
9: **if** (r.$\mathcal{P}$-$\mathcal{Q}$) <> $\emptyset$) {the current node provides more than required}
10:    N = get_Has_of_Children(r);
11:    **for all** ($n \in$ N)
12:       S=HQ(n, $\mathcal{Q}$; {the search will be performed on the Has-Of children}
13:       **if** (S <>NULL) **return** S;
14:    **return** NULL;

There is an assumption of this approach. That is, there is no *confusing nodes* in an ontology tree. A confusing node is the one that is a has-of child of another node and it also has is-a children. The confusing node may cause the potential desired node to be ignored due to the heuristic pruning. For example, in the tree depicted in Figure 2.5, node 7 is a has-of child of node 3 and it has an is-a child node 13. Suppose that we want to find a node that provides {a, k} (i.e., node 13). We cannot find the node following the process in Algorithm 1 since node 13 is unreachable.

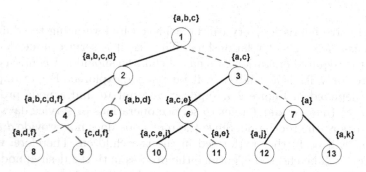

Fig. 2.5   Another ontology tree

Allowing confusing nodes in a Web service ontology tree will improve the flexibility of designing the service ontology. It can also make the ontology structure more intuitive for understanding. Therefore, the proposed query scheme is quite limited. To address the limitation, we first identify the confusing nodes in an ontology tree. We then modify the heuristic query process to ensure that the potential desired node won't be missed.

Algorithm 2 shows the steps of identifying confusing node by coloring the ontology tree. The tree nodes are initially *white*. If a node is identified as a confusing node, it will be colored red. The coloring process starts at the root node. All the has-of children of the current node will be colored *pink*, showing that they are the potential confusing node (Lines 5-6). If a *pink* node also has is-a children, it is then identified as a confusing node and colored *red* (Lines 7-8). Once a node is colored red, its parents will also be colored *red* to ensure that the confusing node won't be ignored during the query process (Lines 11-13).

Algorithm 2 Tree Coloring

1: Initially, all the nodes in the tree are colored *white*
2: **Procedure** Color_Tree(r)
3: N_i=get_Is_a_Children(r);
4: N_h=get_Has_of_Children(r);
5: **for all** $(n \in N_h)$
6:    n.color=*pink*; Color_Tree(n);
7: **if** (r.color==*pink*) **and** $(N_i <> \emptyset)$
8:    Red_Color(r)
9:    **for all** $(n \in N_i)$
10:      Color_Tree(n);
11: **Procedure** Red_Color(r)
12: r.color=red; n=get_Parent(r);
13: **if** (n.color <> red) Red_Color(n);

Figure 2.6 shows the result of applying Algorithm 2 to the ontology tree.

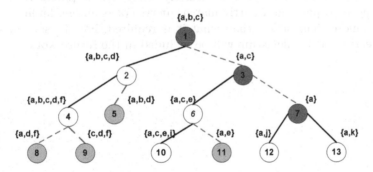

Fig. 2.6 The colored ontology tree

Algorithm 3 shows the steps of the querying the colored tree. The heuristic query process is modified to ensure that the desirable node will be located with the existence of confusing nodes. For the *white*-colored or *pink*-colored nodes, the query process is performed in the similar way as in Algorithm 1. The difference is, for the red-colored node, the query will be performed on both is-a and has-of Children of the node (Lines 3-8). The advanced query process keeps the heuristic by pruning the search space for non red-colored nodes, as well as ensures the reachability of any targeted nodes.

Algorithm 3 Advanced Heuristic Query

1: **Function** IHQ(r, $\mathcal{Q}$) {r is a service node, $\mathcal{Q}$ is a set of required operations or data}
2: **if** (r.$\mathcal{P}$ == $\mathcal{Q}$) **return** r; {find the match}
3: **if** (r.color==red) {the current node is a confusing node}
4:      N =getr_all_Children(r);
5:      **for all** ($n \in N$)
6:          S=IHQ(n, $\mathcal{Q}$); {the search will be performed on all children}
7:          **if** S <> NULL **return** S;
8:      **return** NULL;
9: **if** (($\mathcal{Q}$-r.$\mathcal{P}$) <> $\emptyset$){the current node does not cover the required set}
10:     N = get_Is_a_Children(r);
11:     **for all** ($n \in$ N)
12:         S=HQ(n, $\mathcal{Q}$); {the search will be performed on the is-a children}
13:         **if** (S <>NULL) **return** S;
14:     **return** NULL;
15: **if** (r.$\mathcal{P}$-$\mathcal{Q}$) <> $\emptyset$) {the current node provides more than required}
16:     N = get_Has_of_Children(r);
17:     **for all** ($n \in$ N)
18:         S=HQ(n, $\mathcal{Q}$; {the search will be performed on the Has-Of children}
19:         **if** (S <>NULL) **return** S;
20:     **return** NULL;

The proposed query process can be used to perform an exact-match query, i.e., looking for the node provides exactly what it is required. It can also be extended to perform a partly-match query. For example, finding a node provides more than or less than what it is required. For the sake of space, the extension of the algorithm will be included in the future work.

Chapter 3
A Supporting Infrastructure of a LCS

In this chapter, we propose a supporting infrastructure of a LCS. We first give an overview of a LCS's architecture. It mainly consists of two key components: *LCS schema* and *LCS instance*. It also contains two supporting components: *ontology providers* and *Web service providers*. A LCS schema is the kernel of a LCS since it defines its high-level business logic. It guides the composition of outsourced Web services to perform the functionality of the LCS. We give the formal definition and analyze the *correctness* of the schema.

3.1 An Overview of a LCS

Figure 3.1 depicts the architecture of a LCS. There are two key components and two supporting components in this architecture. The key components include a *LCS schema* and a *LCS instance*. The two supporting components include *ontology providers* and *Web service providers*.

- *LCS schema:* A LCS schema consists of a set of abstract services and the relationships among these services. An abstract service specifies one type of functionality provided by the Web services. They are not bounded to any concrete services. They are defined in terms of service concepts in a Web service ontology.
- *LCS instance:* A LCS instance is a composition of a set of concrete services, which instantiates a LCS schema. It actually delivers the functionality and performance of a LCS.
- *Ontology providers:* The ontology provider manages and maintains a set of ontologies that describe the semantics of Web services. A LCS outsources semantics from an ontology provider to build up its schema.
- *Web service providers:* The Web service providers offer a set of Web services, which can be outsourced to form LCS instances.

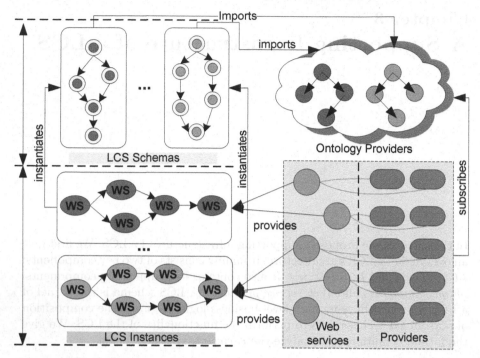

Fig. 3.1 The architecture of a LCS

The underpinning of the proposed LCS architecture is a standard *Service Oriented Architecture* (SOA)[1]. The service providers use WSDL to describe Web services [92]. The WSDL description specifies the address and the arguments to invoke the service. Web service registries, such as UDDI, can be used as a directory for a LCS to look for Web services [91]. After locating a Web service, SOAP messages are exchanged between a LCS and the service providers for invoking the service [90]. Beyond this, semantic Web service technologies can be used by the ontology providers to define their service ontology, such as OWL-S and WSMO [23, 96]. The composition between selected services can be defined using service orchestration languages, such as BPEL [51].

---

[1] http://webservices.xml.com/pub/a/ws/2003/09/30/soa.html

3.2 LCS Schema

A LCS can be considered as a special type of Web services. It then has the similar features as Web services, which include *functionality* (i.e., what it offers), *quality* (i.e., quality), and *context* (i.e., under what environment). The difference between a LCS and common Web services lies in that a LCS outsources its functionality from third-party service providers, instead of providing the functionality by itself. Therefore, it also needs to capture the collaboration between the outsourced Web services within a LCS.

A LCS schema is the basis for specifying a change. Moreover, once there is a change required to be made to a LCS, such as its functionality, it will be more efficient to start at the schema level then directly go to the instance-level where concrete Web services and detailed orchestration are concerned. In this section, we define a LCS schema, which describes a LCS's features at a high-level. We use a *schema graph* to capture the functionality of a LCS as well as the collaboration between the outsourced services. We then formally define the other two features of a LCS: quality and context.

3.2.1 Schema Graph

A LCS outsources its functionality from individual and autonomous services. Therefore, its functionality can be specified by two types of information: (1) the services it outsources (2) the composition of the services. It is worth to note that Web services are *autonomous* and *independent*. They may change their features, or come and go at their will. Considering this dynamic situation, we define a LCS's functionality using a set of *abstract services* (i.e., the service concepts in a Web service ontology), instead of using concrete Web services. Each abstract service corresponds to one type of functionality, such as airline service, or hotel service. The composition of different services specifies how they affect each other by exchanging messages. It can be defined in terms of a *data flow* and a *control flow*. The data flow specifies the data transfer between different services. The control flow specifies the invocation order among the services. Therefore, we can use a directed graph (DG) to define a LCS schema, where nodes represent abstract services and edges represent the data flows and the control flows. In particular, we define a LCS's functionality (referred to as *schema graph*) as follows.

Definition 3.1: A LCS schema graph is the directed graph that has two types of edges $DG=\{N, DE, CE\}$, where:

N is a set of nodes. $N=\{n_\epsilon, n_1, n_2, ..., n_n, n_\omega\}$, where n_ϵ and n_ω are two special nodes that represent the user of the LCS. n_ϵ only has outgoing edges and n_ω only has incoming edges. n_i represents an abstract service $(1 \leq i \leq n)$.

DE is a set of edges. $DE=\{de_1, de_2, ..., de_s\}$, where $de_i=\{n_f, n_t, d_i\}$ represents that n_f sends a message containing data d_i to n_t. $n_f, n_t \in N$. If n_f is

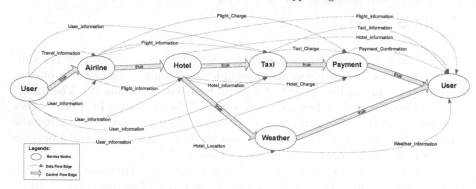

Fig. 3.2 An example of a LCS schema graph

n_ϵ, it means the data d_i is part of the input of a LCS getting from the users. If n_t is n_ω, it means the data d_i is part of the output of a LCS returning to the users.

CE is a set of edges. $CE=\{ce_1, ce_2, ..., ce_t\}$, where $ce_i=\{n_b, n_a, c_i\}$ represents that n_a will be invoked after n_b is invoked if condition c_i is fulfilled. $n_b, n_a \in N$. If n_b is n_ϵ, it means that the invocation of the LCS starts from invoking n_a. If n_a is n_ω, it means that the invocation of the LCS ends with invoking n_b.

Figure 3.2 shows the schema of the travel agency LCS in our running example. The LCS provides a comprehensive travel package by outsourcing functionality from an Airline service, a Hotel service, a Taxi service, a Weather service, and a Payment service. Users are expected to provide their personal information (i.e., user_information), such as their names and billing addresses. They also need to provide the trip information (i.e., travel_information), such as the departure date, arrival date, departure place, and arrival place. An Airline service will be invoked first. After that, it will send the flight information to the Hotel service and the Taxi service. The hotel service will be invoked. After that, it will send its output which contains the hotel Location information to the Taxi service. The Taxi service will take the arrival time of the flight, the location of the airport, and the location of the hotel as input. It then processes the taxi reservation which contains the reservation time and the fee based on the input. After that, the Payment service will be invoked. It receives the data from the three services (i.e., the Airline, Taxi, and Hotel services) generating the fee information from each of them and charges the payment. It then generates the payment confirmation information which will be returned to the user. The Weather service will be invoked after the invocation of the Hotel service since it will take the hotel location and reservation time as its input and generate the weather information as its output.

3.2.2 LCS Quality

The quality of a LCS consists of a set of quality parameters, such as *reliability*, *fee*, *invocation duration*, and *reliability*. These parameters constitute a quality model that is used to evaluate *how well* a LCS performs. The quality model is *domain-specific*. A LCS outsources its functionality from multiple services. Meanwhile, it also outsources quality models from these services. Therefore, we define a LCS's quality model as follows.

Definition 3.2 LCS Quality: *A LCS's quality is a set* $Q =$ $\{q_1, q_2, ..., q_n\}$, *where* q_i *is a quality parameter. Meanwhile* $Q \in$ $(\bigcup_{n_i \in N} n_i.Q)$.

Since a LCS's quality is actually delivered by the Web services it outsources, the quality thus can be determined by these services. Since a LCS instance contains multiple services, we need to aggregate the QoWS parameters from different services. Table 3.1 lists the aggregate functions for the QoWS parameters.

Table 3.1 QoWS for a LCS instance

QoWS parameter	Aggregation function
Latency	$\sum_{i=1}^{n} latency(ws_i)$
Reliability	$\prod_{i=1}^{n} rel(ws_i)$
Availability	$\prod_{i=1}^{n} av(ws_i)$
Fee	$\sum_{i=1}^{n} fee(ws_i)$
Encryption	$\frac{1}{n} \sum_{i=1}^{n} enc(ws_i)$
Authentication	$\frac{1}{n} \sum_{i=1}^{n} aut(ws_i)$
Non-repudiation	$\frac{1}{n} \sum_{i=1}^{n} nrep(ws_i)$
Confidentiality	$\frac{1}{n} \sum_{i=1}^{n} con(ws_i)$

3.2.3 LCS Context

The context of a LCS consists of a set of context types, such as *location*, *time*, *user*, and *travel type*. The context types structure the environment that affects how a LCS performs its functionality. They contain important information for the interaction between a LCS and its users. Since a LCS outsources its functionality from multiple services, its context structure can be determined by these services. Therefore, we define a LCS's context as follows.

Definition 3.3 LCS Context: *A LCS's context is a set* $C =$ $\{c_1, c_2, ..., c_n\}$, *where* c_i *is a context type. Meanwhile* $C \in (\bigcup_{n_i \in N} n_i.C)$.

3.3 Schema Correctness

A LCS schema defines its *configuration* with respect to its functionality. It needs to be *correct* so that the LCS can function well. For example, an outsourced service should make a direct or indirect contribution to the overall functionality of a LCS. Otherwise, it will be meaningless to be included. It should be guaranteed that it can retrieve all its required input to be invoked. In this section, we define a set of criteria for a LCS schema from both *structural* and *semantic correctness* perspectives.

3.3.1 Structural Correctness

We define a LCS's functionality as a directed graph, which consists of a set of nodes and two types of edges. From a *structural* point of view, we define the correctness of a LCS as follows.

Correctness Criterion 1 – *Let M be a LCS schema. If there is a node $n \in M.DG.N$ and n does not have any incoming or outgoing edges, M is not a correct schema.*

The criterion means that there should not be any isolated node in a LCS schema graph. A LCS schema contains two sets of edges: DE and CE. These edges reflect the relationships between different services, i.e., how they are combined together. If there is a node that is not connected to any other node, the node has no interactions with others. Therefore, the LCS schema is incorrect.

Correctness Criterion 2 – *Let M be a LCS schema. If there is a node $n \in M.DG.N$ and there is not an edge e, where $e \in M.DG.CE$ and e goes to n, M is not a correct schema.*

The criterion means that there should not be any node in a LCS schema graph that there is no incoming CE edge. Edges in CE show the invocation order among different services. An incoming CE edge of a node n means that n should be invoked after the invocation of the node where the edge comes from. For a service that needs to be invoked first, it will have an incoming CE edge comes from n_ϵ, which represents the user of the LCS. Therefore, if a node does not have a CE incoming edge, it cannot be invoked. In this case, the LCS schema is incorrect.

Correctness Criterion 3 – *Let M be a LCS's schema. If there is a node $n \in M.DG.N$ and there is not an edge e, where $e \in M.DG.DE$ and e comes from n, M is not a correct schema.*

The criterion means that there should not be any node in a LCS schema graph that there is no DE edge that comes from it. Edges in DE show the data transfer among different services. An incoming DE edge of a node n shows that n will get input from the node where the edge comes from. An outgoing DE edge of n shows that n will generate the output and send it or part of it to the node where the edge goes to. Each service in a LCS should make a direct or indirect contribution to the overall output of a LCS. Therefore, a node should send its output to other services or the user of a LCS (i.e., n_ω). Otherwise, $\mathcal{M}$ is not a correct schema.

3.3.2 Semantic Correctness

Each node represents an abstract service in a LCS schema graph. The abstract services are described by a Web service ontology. The ontology contains sufficient semantics such as the input/output of a Web service for automatic service description, discovery, and composition [23, 96]. A LCS schema should be correct from the *semantic* point of view. We define the semantic correctness as follows.

Correctness Criterion 4 – *Let $\mathcal{M}$ be a LCS schema. If there is a node $n_i \in \mathcal{M}.DG.N$ and one of its input data item d does not be fed by other nodes, $\mathcal{M}$ is not a correct schema.*

The criterion means that each service in a LCS should have all its input fed by other services or the user of the LCS. Otherwise, the LCS schema is not a correct schema. A service is expected to be invoked by a set of messages, which contain the necessary information for the invocation. For example, the information about the date and location is always required to access an airline service. Therefore, the input of a service should be covered by its incoming DE messages so that it can be invoked. Otherwise, $\mathcal{M}$ is not a correct schema.

Correctness Criterion 5 – *Let $\mathcal{M}$ be a LCS schema. If there is a DE edge between n_i and n_j, there should be a CE path between n_i and n_j. Otherwise, $\mathcal{M}$ is not a correct schema.*

The criterion means that the control flow should be consistent with the data flow. If a node n_i needs an input from another node n_j, the invocation of n_i should depend on the invocation of n_j. There are two basic types of service compositions: *horizontally* and *vertically* [61]. If n_i and n_j are combined horizontally, the invocation of n_i should be after the completion of the invocation of n_j. If n_i and n_j are combined horizontally, n_i and n_j need input from each other. In this case, there should be an invocation cycle between n_i and n_j. n_i may be first invoked, it then send messages to n_j and n_j will be invoked. After that, n_j will generate output and send messages to n_i. n_i will continue to be invoked. $\mathcal{M}$ should guarantee that the order of data transfer and service invocation are the same. Otherwise, it is not a correct schema.

The summary of the above criteria is depicted as Table 3.2.

Table 3.2 The LCS schema correctness criteria

id	Type	Description
1	structural	$(\exists n)((n \in \mathcal{M}.DG.N) \wedge \neg(\exists e)((e \in (\mathcal{M}.DG.DE \vee \mathcal{M}.DE.CE)) \wedge ((e.from = n) \vee (e.to = n)))) \Rightarrow \mathcal{M}$ is not a correct schema.
2	structural	$(\exists n)((n \in \mathcal{M}.DG.N) \wedge \neg(\exists e)((e \in \mathcal{M}.DG.CE) \wedge (e.to = n))) \Rightarrow \mathcal{M}$ is not a correct schema.
3	structural	$(\exists n)((n \in \mathcal{M}.DG.N) \wedge \neg(\exists e)((e \in \mathcal{M}.DG.DE) \wedge (e.from = n))) \Rightarrow \mathcal{M}$ is not a correct schema.
4	semantic	$(\exists n)((n \in \mathcal{M}.DG.N) \wedge (\exists d)(d \in n.input) \wedge \neg(\exists e)((e \in \mathcal{M}.DG.DE) \wedge ((e.to = n) \wedge (d \in e.data))) \Rightarrow \mathcal{M}$ is not a correct schema.
5	semantic	$(\exists e)((e \in \mathcal{M}.DG.CE) \wedge \neg(\exists p)((p \in Path(\mathcal{M}.DG.DE)) \wedge (p.start = e.from) \wedge (p.end = e.to))) \Rightarrow \mathcal{M}$ is not a correct schema.

Chapter 4
Top-down Change Language

Top-down changes need to be machine comprehensible so that they can be automatically and correctly enacted. Therefore, top-down change specification should achieve the following: (1) It should be *unambiguous* about what a change intends to be implemented. (2) It should be *formal* so that it can be processed by machines. (3) It should be *disciplined* to ensure that sufficient information is provided. In this chapter, we present a formal language, the *Service Change Management Language* (SCML), to specify top-down changes. Since a change introduces new requirements on the LCS's features, we first present a taxonomy that classifies top-down changes based on their requirements. The taxonomy is built on top of the proposed LCS schema. Based on the change taxonomy, we then present the SCML that enables the formal specification of changes.

4.1 Change Taxonomy

A primary task to manage top-down changes in a LCS is to identify a clear classification of these changes. Thus, different reaction policies can be developed to deal with different types of changes. As depicted in Figure 4.1, we use *change requirement* as a dimension to classify changes. The change requirement reflects the purpose of introducing a change, which could be a result of business policies, business regulations, laws, or just the intension of LCS owners.

Using change requirement as a dimension, changes can be classified based on the key features of a LCS. This conforms to the classical change taxonomy approaches from the fields of software engineering and workflow systems [83, 59]. A LCS outsources the functionality from multiple Web services. Each component service offers a type of functionality. A long-term relationship is formed among the component services for their cooperation. The features of a LCS can be classified into *functional* and *non-functional*.

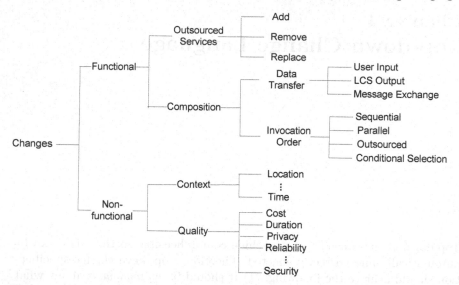

Fig. 4.1   A taxonomy of top-down changes in a LCS

The functional feature refers to the *functionality* of a LCS. The non-functional features include *context* and *quality*. Top-down changes are expected to modify one or more of the features of a LCS. Therefore, we classify changes based on these features. We elaborate on each type of changes as follows.

4.1.1 Functional Changes

Functional changes are those that require to modify the functionality of a LCS. A LCS's functionality is specified by two types of information: the *abstract services* it outsources and their *composition*.

4.1.1.1 Changes of Abstract Services

A LCS may change the type of services it outsources for the purpose of enacting a business policy. The change includes *adding, removing*, and *replacing* a functionality. This could happen for the purpose of fulfilling three types of requirements: *functional requirements*, *context type requirements*, and *quality model requirements*.

Functional Requirement: A LCS's outsourced services may be changed to fulfill a functional requirement. It can be adding a service to the business model to enrich its functionality. For example, a travel agency may need to outsource a Point-Of-Interest (POI) service to attract more customers. A

LCS may also want to remove a service from its business model. For example, consider that a travel agency LCS may outsource an airline service, a hotel service, a train service, a taxi service, and a car rental service. Suppose that the train service does not make satisfactory profit for the LCS. In this case, it may need to be removed from the LCS. A LCS may also want to replace a service in its business model. For example, a travel agency LCS may use an online payment system for reserving a trip. The payment system only supports online bank wire transfer. Considering that users may prefer to use credit card for online transactions, a credit card supported payment service will be used to replace the original one.

As we defined in a Web service ontology, a functionality has two facets: *operations* and *data*. For the first facet, the intended service should provide the specified operations. An example of such a change is "adding a service that provides flight status checking operation". For the second facet, the intended service should provide the ability of transducing data. Put differently, it should be able to generate the specified output by using the given input. An example of such a change is "adding a service that can generate the weather information given a zip code". We define a functional requirement as follows.

Definition 4.1 Functional Requirement: *A functional requirement (f) is a triplet (OP, D_I, D_O), where OP is a set of operations that a service should provide, D_I and D_O are two sets of data items stating that a service should be able to generate D_O by using D_I.*

Context Type Requirement: A LCS's outsourced services may be changed due to a new context type requirement. Each abstract service is associated with a set of context types, which constitute the environment structure of the service. Suppose that a LCS is required to support a new context, such as history data. It then needs to ensure that each outsourced service is able to embed the history data information in the SOAP message during the interactions. This may trigger the change of "removing the service that does not support a context type of history data".

Quality Model Requirement: A LCS's outsourced services may be changed due to a new quality requirement. Each abstract service is associated with a quality model, which includes the parameters for service evaluation. For example, a top-down change may require a new quality parameter to evaluate the outsourced services, such as privacy. This may trigger the change of "removing the service that does not include privacy in its quality model".

Definition 4.2 LCS outsourced abstract service change: *An outsourced functionality change of a LCS (FM) is a triplet $\{F^+, F^-, F^R\}$, where F^+ is a set of abstract services representing the functionality that will be added to the LCS, F^- is a set of abstract services representing the functionality that will be deleted from the LCS, and F^R is a set of abstract service pairs. Each pair $<s,s'>$ corresponds to a service replacement, where s will be replaced by s'.*

4.1.1.2 Changes of Service Composition

A LCS's composition defines *how* it performs its functionality. It specifies the coordination of the outsourced services in a LCS.

A LCS's composition may change under two situations. First, when a new service is added to a LCS or a service is deleted from a LCS, a composition change will be introduced. For example, when adding a payment service to a travel agency LCS, it needs to be combined with other services. Second, a LCS's owner may want to change the way that the component services are combined together for some purpose, such as optimization. For example, suppose that a hotel service and a car rental service are invoked sequentially. There is no invocation dependency between them since they do not exchange messages with each other. In this case, the LCS's owner may want to parallelize their invocation to decrease the overall duration time.

The change to a LCS's composition can occur to both *data transfer* and *invocation order*.

Change to data transfer among services includes the modification of *user input, LCS output, adding* or *deleting* a message between two services.

- *User input:* The user input is obtained from the user of a LCS. It contains the information that is necessary to invoke the services outsourced by the LCS. Once there is a change on the outsourced services, a change of the user input may be introduced. For example, when adding a car rental service, some information is required from the user to invoke the service, such as the car type (i.e., full size, compact, mid-size, or economy). A change of the user input may also be introduced by a LCS's owner. For example, a travel agency LCS provides the airline+hotel package. In this package, the information about location and check in/out time is typically determined by the result of invoking the airline service. The owner may now want to change it by letting users provide these information. In this way, users can have more options when they choose their hotels.
- *LCS output:* The LCS output is generated by a LCS and returned to its users. It is contributed directly or indirectly by the services that the LCS outsources from. Once there is a change of the outsourced services, a change of the LCS output may be introduced. For example, when adding a car rental service, the LCS will generate more information, such as the pick up/drop off location, time, date, and charges. A change of LCS output may also be introduced by a LCS's owner. For example, a travel agency LCS is used to generate the weather information. The owner may want to stop providing such information in the future.
- *Message exchange:* The message exchange is performed between outsourced services in a LCS. A Web service is interacted by its users or partners completely by message exchange. It is invoked by an input message and reacts to the message with an output message. We define a message as follows.

Definition 4.3 Message: *A message (m) is a tuple $\{s^f, s^t, D\}$, where s^f is the service that the data comes from, s^t is the service that the data goes to, and D is a set of data items delivered.*

Once there is a change of the outsourced services, a change of the message exchange between services may be introduced. For example, when adding a traffic service to a travel package, the LCS owner may want to add the message exchanges from the airline service and the hotel service to the traffic service so that it can generate the corresponding driving direction between the airport to the hotel.

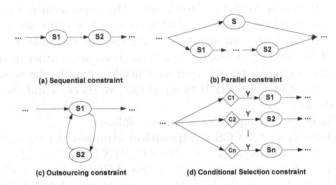

(a) Sequential constraint   (b) Parallel constraint

(c) Outsourcing constraint   (d) Conditional Selection constraint

Fig. 4.2 Four types of process constraints

Changes to the invocation order refer to *adding* a process constraint, which can be *sequential, parallel, outsourcing,* or *conditional selection*. Figure 4.2 shows these four types of process constraints. Their definitions are given as below.

Definition 4.4 Process Constraints: *A process constraint (p) can be either one of the follows:*

- *Sequential Constraint: $P^{>>}(s_1, s_2)$ means that s_1 is invoked before the invocation of s_2. It usually exists between two services where one service requires the result of another service's invocation.*
- *Parallel Constraint: $P^{||}(s, s_1, s_2)$ means that s's invocation is in parallel with the invocation block from s_1 and s_2. It usually exists between the services where there are no message exchanges between them.*
- *Outsourcing Constraint: $P^{\dashv}(s_1, s_2)$ means that s_1 outsources functionality from s_2. It usually exists between two services where a service's (i.e., s_2's) invocation is totally embedded in another service's (i.e., s_1's) invocation. For the sake of simplicity and without the loss of generality, we assume that s_2 does not have any interaction with other services in a LCS than s_1.*
- *Conditional Selection Constraint: $P^?((c_1, s_1), ..., (c_n, s_n))$ means that if c_i is fulfilled, s_i will be invoked, where $1 \leq i \leq n$. It always exists among*

different services which provide the similar functionality in a coarse granularity. Examples of such functionality include taxi services and car rental services, which both provide the ground transporation.

Adding a new service will naturally introduce the changes to the invocation order among component services in a LCS. The invocation order between the new service and the other services may be specified by the owner of a LCS. It is worth to note that some invocation order for new services can also be automatically generated. It will be determined by the owner of a LCS whether it is necessary to specify the invocation order for new services or not. For the changes of the invocation order between two existing services, "adding" actually does a "replacing" work here. More specifically, when adding a new process constraint on the invocation order between two services, the previous one will be deleted to avoid the conflicts. For example, if the owner of an travel agency LCS wants to change the invocation order of the hotel service and the car rental service from sequential to parallel, he needs to first delete the sequential constraint between these two services and then add a parallel constraint.

We define a composition change as follows.

Definition 4.5 LCS composition change: *A composition change of a LCS (FM) is a tuple* $\{I^+, I^-, O^+, O^-, MX^+, MX^-, P^+\}$, *where* I^+ *is a set of input data that will be added to the LCS,* I^- *is a set of input data that will be deleted from the LCS,* O^+ *is a set of output data that will be added to the LCS,* O^- *is a set of output data that will be deleted from the LCS,* MX^+ *is a set of data transfers that will be added to the LCS,* MX^- *is a set of data transfers that will be deleted from the LCS, and* P^+ *is a set of process constraints that will be added to the LCS.*

4.1.2 Non-functional changes

Non-functional changes are those that require to change the non-functional features of a LCS, including *context* and *performance* changes.

The context of a LCS specifies its environmental information. It can be any meta-data that is related to the interactions between the LCS and its users, such as location, time, and payment methods. A top-down change may require to change the context of its component services. For example, in a travel agency LCS, the taxi service is located in the US. Suppose users tend to use the taxi service when they travel in Europe. The LCS's owner may want to change the location of the taxi service it outsources to Europe to better serve its users' needs. The result of this change may be a replacement of the concrete taxi service in the LCS. For another example, in the LCS, the hotel service only accepts credit card payment. Suppose users tend to use other payment methods, such as paypal. The LCS's owner may want to change the payment method of the hotel service it outsources accordingly. The result

of this change may be that the LCS's owner will find another hotel service
which satisfies the new context requirement to replace the previous one. We
define a context change as follows.

Definition 4.6 LCS Context Change: *A context change of a LCS
(CM) is a set* $\{\lambda_1, \lambda_2, ..., \lambda_m\}$*, where* λ_i *is a context constraint that is enforced
on the outsourced services. It can be specified as* $\{S, e, v\}$*, where* S *is a set
of outsourced abstract service of a LCS, e specifies the context type, and* v
specifies the new value of the context.

The quality of a LCS refers to its non-functional features, such as its
reliability, fee, invocation duration, and reputation. It evaluates the quality
delivered by a LCS. A top-down change may require to modify the quality
that a LCS delivers. For example, a LCS's owner may want to guarantee that
the providers of its component services should have a decent reputation. We
define a quality change as follows.

Definition 4.7 LCS Quality Change: *A quality change of a LCS (QM)
is a set* $\{\delta_1, \delta_2, ..., \delta_n\}$*, where* δ_i *is a quality constraint that is enforced on
the outsourced services. It can be specified as* $\{S, i, r\}$*, where* S *is a set of
outsourced services of a LCS, i specifies the quality parameter, and* r *indicates
the requirement on these services with respect to i.*

A top-down change can be thus modeled as the modification of the LCS's
features, where we summarize in Table 4.1.

Table 4.1 Top-down change model

Top-down Changes	Definition
Outsourced Abstract Services Change	$FM = (F^+, F^-, F^R)$.
Composition Change	$OM = (O^+, O^-, I^+, I^-, M^+, M^-, P^+)$.
Context Change	$CM = (\lambda_1, \lambda_2, ..., \lambda_m)$.
Quality Change	$QM = (\delta_1, \delta_2, ..., \delta_n)$.

4.2 Change Operators

Based on the proposed change taxonomy, we present two types of *change
operators*: *functional* and *non-functional*. We elaborate on these operators in
the sequel.

4.2.1 Functional Change Operators

The functionality changes may occur to a LCS's outsourced abstract services (FM) and their composition (OM). We use M to denote a LCS's schema. FM consists of three sets, including the abstract services that are intended to be added (F^+), removed (F^-), and replaced (F^R). The selection of these abstract services is based on the three types of requirements: functional requirement, context type requirement, and quality model requirement. Therefore, we define the change operators for selecting abstract services as follows.

- $\Pi_{op}^F(op, O)$: It will traverse the service ontology O to find the abstract services that provide the specified operation op. This operator takes op and O as input and returns an abstract service.
- $\Pi_d^F(D_I, D_O, O)$: It will traverse the service ontology O to find the abstract services that can generate the required output of D_O by using the given input D_I. This operator takes two sets of data, D_I, D_O as well as a service ontology O as input and returns an abstract service.
- $\Pi^C(c, O)$: It will traverse the service ontology O to find the abstract services that support a context type c. This operator takes c and O as input and returns a list of abstract services.
- $\Pi^Q(q, O)$: It will traverse the service ontology O to find the abstract services that include a quality parameter q in its quality model. This operator takes s and q as input and returns a list of abstract services.

For the selected service node, we define two change operators as below.

- $\triangle^S$ (s, O, M, op): It will perform the operation op, by either *adding* or *removing* an abstract service to or from a LCS's schema M. This operator takes s, M, and op as input and returns a new LCS schema as its output.
- $\triangle^{S\leftrightarrow}$ (s_{old}, s_{new}, O, M): It will replace an abstract service s_{old} with another abstract service s_{new} in a LCS' schema M. This operator takes s_{old}, s_{new}, O, and M as input and returns a new LCS schema as its output.

OM consists of several sets, including a set of input data that is intended to be added (I^+) or removed (I^-), a set of output data that is intended to be added (O^+) or removed (O^-), a set of data transfers that are intended to be added (MX^+) or be removed (MX^-), a set of process constraints that are intended to be added (P^+). Therefore, we define the following change operators for them.

- $\triangle^I$ (M, D, op): It will perform the operation op, by either *adding* the data items in D to or *removing* some data items from a LCS's input.
- $\triangle^O$ (M, D, op): It will perform the operation op, by either *adding* the data items in D to or *removing* some data items from a LCS's output.
- $\triangle^{MX}$ (m, M, op): It will perform the operation op, by either *adding* or *removing* a data transfer m to or from a LCS's schema M. This operator takes m, M, and op as its input and returns a new schema as its output.

- $\Delta_P^{>>}(s_1, s_2, M)$: It will add a sequential constraint on the invocation order defined in M. This operator takes s_1, s_2, M, as its input and returns a new schema as its output.
- $\Delta_P^{||}(s, s_1, s_2, M)$: It will add a parallel constraint on the invocation order defined in M. This operator takes s, s_1, s_2, M as its input and returns a new schema as its output.
- $\Delta_P^{\dashv}(s_1, s_2, M)$: It will add an outsourcing constraint on the invocation order defined in M. This operator takes s_1, s_2, M, op as its input and returns a new schema as its output.
- $\Delta_P^?(s, C, S, M)$: It will add a conditional selection constraint on the invocation order defined in M. C is a set of condition expression and S is a set of services. C and S have the same cardinality. This operator takes C, S, M, op as its input and returns a new schema as its output.

4.2.2 Non-functional Change Operators

The non-functional changes include *context change* (CM) and *quality change* (QM). CM consists of a set of context constraints. QM consists of a set of quality constraints. We define two change operators for these two types of changes: $\Delta^{CM}(\lambda, M)$ and $\Delta^{QM}(\delta, M)$.

- $\Delta^{CM}(\lambda, M)$ It will enforce a context constraint λ on a LCS with the schema M. λ is a triplet $\{S, v, e\}$, where *the services in $\lambda.S$ should have the value of $\lambda.v$ for the context $\lambda.e$*. This operator takes λ and M as its input and returns a new LCS instance as its output.
- $\Delta^{QM}(\delta, M)$ It will enforce a quality constraint δ on a LCS with the schema M. δ is a triplet $\{S, r, i\}$, where *the services in $\delta.S$ should have the value of $\delta.r$ for the quality parameter $\delta.i$*. This operator takes δ and M as its input and returns a new LCS instance as its output.

4.3 Change Language

We propose a *Web Service Change Management Language* (SCML) for the purpose of managing top-down changes. SCML is a SQL-like language. It defines five types of commands: (1) *create command* for defining a LCS schema; (2) *select command* for querying both abstract services and concrete Web services; (3) *alter command* for specifying functional changes; (4) *update command* for specifying non-functional changes; (5)*drop command* for deleting a LCS schema. The commands are defined and elaborated on in this section.

4.3.1 Create Command

The create command is used to specify a new LCS schema. A LCS schema is given a name using two keywords: **CREATE** and **LCS**. For example, by writing

> **CREATE LCS** travel-agency...

a LCS named as travel-agency is created. A LCS is associated with a Web service ontology from where it outsources semantics. Therefore, the Web service ontology is specified first. We use a keyword **ONTOLOGY** to specify the ontology provider that offers the ontology. For example, by writing

> **ONTOLOGY** o http://.../axis2/services/OntologyAccessWithConfig

a LCS is associated with a ontology service which provides ontological semantics for the LCS.

After that, the abstract services in a LCS is specified. Each abstract service corresponds to a service concept in the Web service ontology. It is then described using the name of the service concept. We use the keyword, **SERVICES**, to specify one or more abstract services. For example, by writing

> **SERVICES** s_a airline, s_t taxi, s_h hotel
>
> **SERVICES** s_p payment

we specify four abstract services for the LCS.

We use a keyword, **CONTROL FLOWS**, to specify one or more control flow edges in a LCS schema graph. Each edge is given a name and a description. The description includes the information about the service node that the edge comes from, the service node the edge goes to, and the condition the edge delivers. For example, by writing

> **CONTROL FLOWS** c1 (s_a, s_h, true), c2 (s_h, s_t, true)

we specify a control flow edge from the airline service to the hotel service.

We use a keyword, **DATA FLOWS**, to specify one or more data flow edges in a LCS schema graph. Each edge is given a name and a description. The description includes the information about the service node that the edge comes from, the service node that the edge goes to, and the data item the edge delivers. For example, by writing

> **DATA FLOWS** d1 $(s_a, s_p, \text{ticket\_price})$,

we specify a data flow edge from the airline service to the payment service with the information of a ticket's price.

Recall that there are two special service nodes: n_ω and n_ϵ, which refer to the user of a LCS. We use a keyword, **USER**, to specify these two service nodes when defining edges in a LCS schema graph. For example, by writing

> **DATA FLOWS** d2 (**USER**, s1, user_Id), d3 (s1, **USER**, flight_schedule)

we specify two data flow edges. In d1, the information is obtained from a LCS's users and sent to the airline service. In d2, the data is generated by the airline service and returned to users.

After specifying a LCS schema graph, we use a keyword, **QUALITIES** to specify one or more quality parameters that are used to evaluate a LCS. A quality parameter is given a name and a description. For example, by writing

QUALITIES q1 availability, q2 cost

we specify two quality parameters.

We use a keyword, **CONTEXTS** to specify one or more contexts of a LCS. A context is given a name and a description. For example, by writing

CONTEXTS c1 location, c2 time, c3 currency

we specify three contexts for the LCS.

Therefore, we can define a LCS schema as follows.

CREATE LCS travel-agency (

ONTOLOGY o http://wsms-dev.csiro.au:8080/axis2/services
/OntologyAccessWithConfig

SERVICES s_a airline, s_t taxi, s_h hotel, s_p payment, s_w weather...

...

CONTROL FLOWS c1 (s_a, s_h, true), c2 (s_h, s_t, true)...

...

DATA FLOWS d1 (s_a, s_p, ticket_price),

...

QUALITIES q1 availability, q2 cost

...

CONTEXTS c1 location, c2 time, c3 currency

...

)

4.3.2 Select Command

The select command is used to specify a query on a Web service ontology. The corresponding change operators include: $\Pi_{op}^F(op, O)$, $\Pi_d^F(D_I, D_O, O)$, $\Pi_C^F(c, O)$, and $\Pi_Q^F(q, O)$. A query can be performed based on the features of a LCS: functional and non-functional. Similar to a select statement in SQL, a SCML select command is formed of the three clauses, which start with three keywords: **SELECT**, **FROM**, and **WHERE**, respectively.

SELECT

FROM <ontology>

WHERE <condition>

where is a list of abstract services that are intended to be retrieved by the query; <ontology> is the Web service ontology that the query is performed upon; and <condition> is a conditional expression (Boolean) that identifies the services to be retrieved by the query. In SCML, a conditional expression has the following format:

<operator><values>

The operators include **hasOperation**, **hasInput**, **hasOutput**, **hasQuality**, and **hasContext**. They are defined for the four change operators that require a query on a Web service ontology. For each of these change operators, we give an example of a SCML query statement.

- $\Pi_{op}^F(op, O)$: **SELECT** s **FROM** o **WHERE** s **hasOperation** (airline_reservation)
- $\Pi_d^F(D_I, D_O, O)$: **SELECT** s **FROM** o **WHERE** s **hasInput** (location, date) **and** s **hasOutput** (weather_information)
- $\Pi_Q^F(q, O)$: **SELECT** s **FROM** o **WHERE** s **hasQuality** (privacy)
- $\Pi_C^F(c, O)$: **SELECT** s **FROM** o **WHERE** s **hasContext** (history_data)

4.3.3 Alter Command

The alter command is used to specify functional changes in a LCS. The possible *alter LCS schema actions* include (1) adding or deleting user input or LCS output, (2) adding, deleting, or replacing abstract services and/or data flow edges), and (3) adding a process constraint.

For (1) and (2), the alter command is formed as:

   ALTER LCS <LCS name> <action> <element type> <value>

where an action can be **ADD**, **DELETE**, or **REPLACE**. An element type can be **INPUT**, **OUTPUT**, **SERVICES**, and **DATA FLOWS**. When the action is **REPLACE**, the element type has to be **SERVICES**. The value type for **REPLACE** action is a pair. For other actions, the value contains a service name and the name of its corresponding service concept in the service ontology . The alter command corresponds to the five functional change operators. We give an example of a SCML alter command for each of them.

- Δ^S (s, O, M, op): **ALTER LCS** travel-agency **ADD SERVICES**(s_f traffic, s_l local_activity, s_z address_to_zip);
- $\Delta^{S \leftrightarrow}$ (s_{old}, s_{new}, O, M): **ALTER LCS** travel agency **REPLACE SERVICES** $(s_t, s_c$ car_rental);
- Δ^I (M, D, op): **ALTER LCS** travel-agency **ADD INPUT** (car_type)
- Δ^O (M, D, op): **ALTER LCS** travel-agency **DELETE OUTPUT** (taxi_charge, taxi_schedule)
- Δ^{MX} (m, M, op): **ALTER LCS** travel-agency **ADD DATA FLOWS** (<USER, s_c, car_type>)

When adding a process constraint, the alter command is formed as:

   ALTER LCS <LCS name> **ADD PROCESS CONSTRAINT** <constraint type><value>

where <constraint type> can be **SEQUENTIAL**, **PARALLEL**, **OUTSOURCING**, and **CONDITIONAL SELECTION**. The four constraint types correspond to the four change operators. We give an example of a SCML alter command for each of them.

- $\Delta_P^{>>}$ (s_1, s_2, M): **ALTER LCS** travel-agency **ADD PROCESS CONSTRAINT SEQUENTIAL** (s_a, s_c);

- $\Delta_P^{\parallel}$ (s, s_1, s_2, M): **ALTER LCS** travel-agency **ADD PROCESS CON-STRAINT PARALLEL** (s_h, s_c, s_c);
- $\Delta_P^{\rightarrow}$ (s_1, s_2, M): **ALTER LCS** travel-agency **ADD PROCESS CONSTRAINT OUTSOURCING** (s_w, s_z);
- $\Delta_P^{?}$ (s, C, S, M): **ALTER LCS** travel-agency **ADD PROCESS CON-STRAINT CONDITIONAL SELECTION** $(s_h,$ <travel_type="international", $s_t>$, <travel_type="domestic", $s_c>$);

4.3.4 Update Command

The update command is used to specify non-functional changes. The possible *update LCS actions* include: (1) changing a LCS quality, and (2) changing a LCS context. When changing a LCS quality, a update command is formed as:

> **UPDATE LCS** <LCS name> **SET** <service list> <quality parameter> <operator> <value>

When changing a LCS context, a update command is formed as:

> **UPDATE LCS** <LCS name> **SET** <service list> <context type> <operator> <value>

The operators can be "=","<","<=",">", ">=", and "<>".

The command corresponds to the two non-functional change operators. We give an example of a SCML update command for each of them.

- Δ^{QM} (δ, M): **UPDATE LCS** travel-agency **SET** (s_a, s_h) **q1="high"**
- Δ^{CM} (λ, M): **UPDATE LCS** travel-agency **SET** (s_t) **c1="European"**

4.3.5 Drop Command

The drop command is used to drop a named LCS schema. We use two key-words: **DROP** and **LCS** to specify a drop command. For example, by writing

> **DROP LCS** travel-agency

we delete the travel agency LCS schema.

4.3.6 Analysis on SCML

SCML needs to achieve the five characteristics to be qualified as a way to model changes in LCSs, including unambiguous, formal, disciplined, complete, and declarative. We give the analysis on SCML with respect to these five characteristics as follows.

SCML is built upon the proposed change taxonomy and change operators. Different types of change operators can be mapped to ALTER and UPDATE commands in SCML. For these commands, different keywords are used to specify the types of the changes and the related parameters. Therefore, a legal SCML statement contains the sufficient information to specify a change, which ensures the change specification to be unambiguous and disciplined.

Predefined keywords are used to constitute an SCML statement. The semantic of these keywords are understandable for machines, such as ALTER, LCS, SELECT, ADD, etc. The semantic of an SCML statement is understandable and processable for machines. Therefore, an SCML change specification is formal.

Each top-down change will fall into one or more categories defined in the change taxonomy. Each change category is mapped to a change operator. Therefore, for a simple change that falls into one change category, it can be specified in term of the corresponding change operator and then be mapped to an SCML statement. For a complex change which falls into more than one change categories, multiple change operators can be used to specify the change. It then can be specified by multiple SCML statement. Therefore, SCML can be used to specify all top-down changes. It is complete.

SCML is SQL-like language. Therefore, it is declarative. For example, if a LCS's owner wants to add a POI service to the LCS, he does not need to provide the operational information, i.e., how to integrate the POI service with other participated services.

Chapter 5
Top-down Change Enactment and Change Optimization

In this chapter, we present a set of algorithms for the processes of enacting and optimizing top down changes. During the process of change enactment, changes are first reacted to at two levels: *schema-level* and *instance-level*. Changes are then verified to ensure the correct configuration of a LCS. The result of change enactment may be multiple new LCS instances. The best one will be chosen during the process of change optimization.

5.1 Change Enactment

Since the kernel of SCML is a set of change operators, we mainly focus on the enactment of these operators. The enactment process consists of four major steps: *selecting service nodes, updating a LCS schema graph, verifying changes*, and *generating the new LCS instance*. Among the change operators, $\Pi_{op}^F(op, O)$, $\Pi_d^F(D_I, D_O, O)$, $\Pi^C(c, s)$, and $\Pi^Q(q, s)$ require the selection of abstract services in terms of service nodes in a service ontology based on a certain requirement, such as *functional, context type*, and *quality model* requirement. The other functional change operators are enacted during the process of generating new LCS schema graphs. A LCS schema is expected to be changed from a *correct* configuration to another *correct* configuration. Therefore, once there is a change to a LCS schema graph, the change needs to be verified. The non-functional change operators are enacted during the process of generating new LCS instances. This process will also be performed after a new correct schema graph is generated.

5.1.1 Select Service Nodes

Selecting service nodes is demanded by four functional change operators: $\Pi_{op}^F(op, O)$, $\Pi_d^F(D_I, D_O, O)$, $\Pi^C(c, O)$, and $\Pi^Q(q, O)$. Implementing these operators is to query the Web service ontology (O) and retrieve the desired service nodes. The service ontology query infrastructure proposed in Chapter 2 can then be leveraged. We elaborate on the process of implementing these operators as follows.

- $\Pi_{op}^F(op, O)$: It requires to find a service node from a service ontology O that fulfills a functional requirement specified by op. The desired services are expected to provide the specified operations (op). It is implemented by performing an operation-based functionality query using names or path expressions, depending on the format of op.
- $\Pi_d^F(D_I, D_O, O)$: It requires to find a service node from a service ontology O that has the ability of generating the specified output using the given input. It is implemented by performing a data-based functionality query on O.
- $\Pi^C(c, s)$ It requires to select services that fulfill a context type requirement specified by c. The desired services are expected to support c. It is implemented by performing a quality-based service query on O.
- $\Pi^Q(q, s)$ It requires to select services that fulfill a quality model requirement specified by q. The desired services are expected to support q. It is implemented by performing a context-based service query on O.

5.1.2 Update LCS schema Graphs

A LCS schema graph will be modified during the process of implementing some functional change operators. These operators include the change to abstract services (i.e., $\triangle^S (s, \mathcal{M}, op)$ and $\triangle^{s\leftrightarrow} (s_{old}, s_{new}, \mathcal{M})$), user input ($\triangle^I (M, D, op)$), LCS output ($\triangle^O (M, D, op)$), message exchanges(i.e., $\triangle^{MX} (m, \mathcal{M}, op)$), and process constraints (i.e., $\triangle_P^{>>} (s_1, s_2, \mathcal{M})$, $\triangle_P^{||} (s, s_1, s_2, \mathcal{M})$, $\triangle_P^{\dashv} (s_1, s_2, \mathcal{M})$, and $\triangle_P^? (s, C, S, \mathcal{M})$). We elaborate on the process of implementing these operators in this section.

Recall that a LCS schema graph consists of three sets. The set N consists of nodes that represent abstract services. The set DE consists of edges that represent data transfers among the services. The set CE consists of edges that define invocation orders among the services. Adding an abstract service is quite straightforward. It can be implemented by simply including the corresponding node to N. Deleting an abstract service can be implemented by performing a node deletion in a graph. The node will be removed from N first. All of its incoming and outgoing edges will then be removed from DE

and CE. Adding or deleting a data transfer is straightforward, too. It can be implemented by simply updating DE.

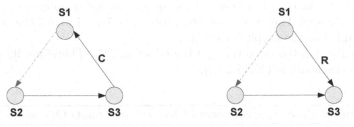

Figure 1: Potential circle   Figure 2: Potential redundancy

Fig. 5.1 The potential conflict and redundancy

The change to process constraints is not as straightforward as implementing other functional change operators. This is because that it may cause the potential conflicts or redundancy of a LCS schema graph, which is depicted in Figure 5.1.

- *Conflict:* The changes of the process constraints may cause conflicts on the invocation orders. As showed in Figure 5.1, there are three services: s_1, s_2, and s_3. s_2 is invoked before s_3 is invoked. s_3 is invoked before s_1. If a sequential process constraint is added to s_1 and s_2, where s_1 is required to be invoked before s_2 is invoked. This implies that s_1 will be invoked before s_3 is invoked. In this case, it will conflict the previous sequential invocation order between s_2 and s_3 and cause an invocation deadlock among these three services.
- *Redundancy:* The changes of the process constraints may also cause redundant edges in CE. As showed in Figure 5.1, s_2 is invoked before s_3 is invoked. s_1 is invoked before s_3 is invoked. If a sequential process constraint is added to s_1 and s_2, the edge from s_1 to s_3 is considered as a *redundant* edge since the invocation order between s_1 and s_3 can be derived from the other two edges.

Considering the above two situations, adding a process constraint needs to follow four steps to update a LCS schema graph: (1) *Map a process constraint to a CE edge* (2) *Check and break the potential circles* (3) *Check and remove the redundant edges* (4) *Add the new CE edges to the schema graph* We will follow these steps when adding the four types of process constraints to a LCS. We elaborate on them as follows.

As showed in Algorithm 4, the first step of implementing $\triangle_P^{>>}(s_1, s_2, \mathcal{M})$ is to map the change operator to the change of CE. That is, a new edge pointing from s_1 to s_2 will be first created (Line 2). After that, it needs to check and fix the potential conflicts made by the change (Line 4 to 6). These edges include the ones pointing from s_2 or s_2's descendent nodes to s_1 or s_1's ancestor nodes. They will be deleted from the graph to avoid the potential deadlock. The next step is to check and remove the redundant edges. These edges include the ones pointing from s_1 or s_1's ancestor nodes to s_2 or s_2's descendent nodes. They will be deleted, too (Line 7-9). Finally, the new edge will be added to the graph (Line 11).

The algorithm traverses through the edges in DE. Therefore, its computational complexity is $O(|\mathcal{M}.CE|)$.

Algorithm 4 Processing Sequential Process Constraints Operators

---

1: Functional change_Parellel_Process_Constraints($s_1, s_2, \mathcal{M}$)
Require: abstract service s_1, s_2, a LCS schema $\mathcal{M}$
Ensure: an updated $\mathcal{M}$
2: $e = (s_1, s_2, true)$; {Step 1: map the process constraint to a CE edge}
3: **for all** $e' \in \mathcal{M}.DG.CE$ **do**
4: **if** $e'.start == \{s_2 \cup s_2.desendent\}$ and $e'.end == \{s_1 \cup s_1.ancestor\}$ **then**
5:    $\mathcal{M}.DG.CE = \mathcal{M}.DG.CE - e$; {Step 2: Check and break the potential circles}
6: **end if**
7: **if** $e'.start \in \{s_1 \cup s_1.ancestor\}$ and $e'.end \in \{s_2 \cup s_2.descendent\}$ **then**
8:    $\mathcal{M}.DG.CE = \mathcal{M}.DG.CE - e$; {Step 3: Check and remove the redundant edges}
9: **end if**
10: **end for**
11: $\mathcal{M}.DG.CE \leftarrow e$ {Step 4: Add the new CE edges to the schema graph}

As showed in Algorithm 5, the first step of implementing $\triangle_P^{||} (s, s_1, s_2, \mathcal{M})$ is to map it to the change of CE. As the definition of parallel constraint, the invocation of s should be in parallel with the invocation block starting from s_1 and s_2. Therefore, s should be invoked after the invocation of the parent nodes of s_1 and before the invocation of the child nodes of s_2. Therefore, the edges pointing from the parent nodes of s_1 to s and the edges pointing from s to the child nodes of s_2 are created. (Line 3 to 10). After that, it needs to check and fix the conflicts made by the change (Line 12 to 17). The conflicting edges include the ones pointing from s or s's descendent nodes to s_1 or s_1's ancestor nodes as well as the ones pointing from s_2 or s_2's decedent nodes to s or s's ancestor nodes. These edges will be deleted from the schema graph. The next step is to check and remove the redundant edges. These edges include the ones pointing from s or s's.ansestor nodes to s_2 or s_2's descendent nodes as well as the ones pointing from s_1 or s_1's ancestor nodes to s or s's decedent nodes. They will be deleted, too (Line 18-22). Finally, the new edges will be added to the graph (Line 25-27).

The algorithm traverses through the edges in DE. Therefore, its computational complexity is $O(|\mathcal{M}.CE|)$.

Algorithm 5 Processing Parallel Process Constraints Operators

---
1: Functional change_Parallel_Constraints($s, s_1, s_2, \mathcal{M}$)
Require: abstract service s, s_1, s_2, a LCS schema $\mathcal{M}$
Ensure: an updated $\mathcal{M}$
2:   $E = \phi$;
3: **for all** $(e \in \mathcal{M}.DG.DE)$ and $(e.end == s_1$ or $e.start == s_2)$ **do**
4:     **if** $e.end == s_1$ **then**
5:        $E \leftarrow (e.start, s, true)$; {Step 1: map the process constraint to CE edges}
6:     **end if**
7:     **if** $e.start = s_2$ **then**
8:        $E \leftarrow (s, e.end, true)$;
9:     **end if**
10: **end for**
11: **for all** $e' \in \mathcal{M}.DG.DE$ **do**
12:    **if** $(e'.start \in \{s$ or s's descedent$\}$ and $e'.end \in \{s_1$ or s_1's ancester$\}$ **then**
13:       $\mathcal{M}.DG.DE = \mathcal{M}.DG.DE - e'$; {Step 2: Check and break the potential circles}
14:    **end if**
15:    **if** $(e'.start \in \{s_2$ or s_2's descedent$\}$ and $e'.end \in \{s$ or s's ancester$\}$ **then**
16:       $\mathcal{M}.DG.DE = \mathcal{M}.DG.DE - e'$;
17:    **end if**
18:    **if** $(e'.start \in \{s$ or s's ancester$\}$ and $e'.end \in \{s_2$ or s_2's descedent$\}$ **then**
19:       $\mathcal{M}.DG.DE = \mathcal{M}.DG.DE - e'$; {Step 3: Check and remove the redundant edges}
20:    **end if**
21:    **if** $(e'.start \in \{s_1$ or s_1's ancester$\}$ and $e'.end \in \{s$ or s's descedent$\}$ **then**
22:       $\mathcal{M}.DG.DE = \mathcal{M}.DG.DE - e'$;
23:    **end if**
24: **end for**
25: **for all** $e \in E$ **do**
26:    $\mathcal{M}.DG.DE \leftarrow (e)$; {Step 4: Add the new CE edges to the schema graph}
27: **end for**

As showed in Algorithm 6, the first step of implementing $\triangle_P^{\rightarrow} (s_1, s_2, \mathcal{M})$ is to map it to the change of CE. In case of adding an outsourcing constraint, s_1 should be invoked first and then trigger the invocation of s_2. s_1's invocation will be pending when s_2 is invoked since it may need the input from s_2. After s_2 is invoked, s_1's invocation will be continued and finished. Therefore, the two corresponding edges will be created and included in CE. One is pointed from s_1 to s_2 and the other is pointed from s_2 to s_1 (Line 3 to 4). These two edges generate a circle in the graph, although they won't cause an invocation order deadlock. Since we assume that s_2 does not have any interactions with other services in LCS except for s_1, adding the oursourcing constraint will not cause any potential conflicts and redundancy. Therefore, we can ignore the step 2 and step 3. The two new edges will be added to DE.

The algorithm generates and adds two edges to CE. Therefore, its computational complexity is $O(1)$.

Algorithm 6 Processing Outsourcing Process Constraints Operators

---
1: Functional change_Outsourcing_Constraints($s_1, s_2, \mathcal{M}, op$)
Require: abstract service s_1, s_2, a LCS schema $\mathcal{M}$ and an add/remove operation op
Ensure: an updated $\mathcal{M}$
2:   $e_1 = (s_1, s_2, true)$; $e_2 = (s_2, s_1, true)$; {Step 1: map the process constraint to CE edges}
3:   $\mathcal{M}.DE.CE \leftarrow e_1, e_2$; {Step 4: Add the new CE edges to the schema graph}

As showed in Algorithm 7, the first step of implementing $\triangle_P^?\,(s,\mathcal{C},\mathcal{S})$ is to map it to the change of CE. As defined by a conditional selection constraint, the services in $\mathcal{S}$ should be invoked after the invocation of s. Each service's invocation will be associated with a condition in $\mathcal{C}$. Therefore, the related edges will be created (Line 3 to 6). The next step is to check and fix the conflicts introduced by the change. The conflicting edges include the ones pointing from the node in $\mathcal{S}$ or its descendent nodes to s or s's ancestor nodes. These edges will be deleted from the schema graph (Line 9 to 11). The next step is to check and remove the redundant edges. These edges include the ones pointing from s or s's.ansestor nodes to the node in $\mathcal{S}$ or its descendent nodes. They will be deleted, too (Line 12-14). Finally, the new edge will be added to the graph (Line 17-19).

The algorithm traverses through the edges in CE and use these edges to check each node in $\mathcal{S}$. Therefore, its computational complexity is $O(|\mathcal{M}.CE|*|\mathcal{S}|)$.

Algorithm 7 Processing Conditional Selection Process Constraints Operators

---

1: Functional change_ConditionalSelection_Process_Constraints($s,\mathcal{C},\mathcal{S},\mathcal{M}$)
Require: abstract service s, an abstract service set $\mathcal{M}$, a condition set$\mathcal{C}$, a LCS schema $\mathcal{M}$
Ensure: an updated $\mathcal{M}$
2:   $E = \phi$
3: **for all** $c_i \in \mathcal{C}$ **do**
4:     $e = (s, s_i, c_i)$; {Step 1: map the process constraint to CE edges}
5:     $E \leftarrow e$;
6: **end for**
7: **for all** ($e \in \mathcal{M}.DG.CE$ **do**
8:     **for all** $s' \in \mathcal{S}$ **do**
9:         **if** e.start $\in \{s'$ or $s'.descedent\}$ AND e.end $\in \{s$ or s's ancestor$\}$ **then**
10:             $\mathcal{M}.DG.CE = \mathcal{M}.DG.CE - e$; {Step 2: Check and break the potential circles}
11:         **end if**
12:         **if** e.start $\in \{s$ or $s.ancestor\}$ AND e.end $\in \{s'$ or s''s decedent$\}$ **then**
13:             $\mathcal{M}.DG.CE = \mathcal{M}.DG.CE - e$; {Step 3: Check and remove the redundant edges}
14:         **end if**
15:     **end for**
16: **end for**
17: **for all** $e \in E$ **do**
18:     $\mathcal{M}.DG.DE \leftarrow (e)$; {Step 4: Add the new CE edges to the schema graph}
19: **end for**

5.1.3 Verify Changes

After a LCS schema graph is changed, it needs to be *verified*. Put differently, the schema graph should maintain its *correct* configuration after a change has been implemented. We define a set of correctness criteria in Chapter 3. The new schema graph needs to conform to these criteria. If not, it needs to be corrected. A schema graph is supposed to be correct before it has been changed. Therefore, we only need to check the nodes that are involved in the change. These nodes include those that are newly added or have edges that have been added or removed. We use N_c to denote these nodes. In this section, we first analyze the impact of verification order on the process of verification. We then elaborate on the whole process of verification.

5.1.3.1 Verification Order

The proposed criteria checks the correctness of a schema graph from two aspects: *structural* and *semantic*. The structural correctness criteria check the incoming and outgoing edges of each nodes. The schema graph should not have any isolated node (criterion 1). It should not have any node that does not have any incoming edge in CE, which ensures that its invocation will be triggered. (criterion 2). The graph also should not have any node that does not have any outgoing edge in DE, which ensures that it will contribute to the output of the LCS directly or indirectly (criterion 3). The semantic correctness criteria check a schema graph from two aspects. First, it needs to check whether the edges in CE ensure that each service gets its input (criterion 4). Second, it needs to compare edges between DE and CE to ensure that the data transfers among the services are consistent with their invocation order (criterion 5). To sum up, the semantic correctness criteria are used to ensure that services can be orchestrated properly. The structural correctness criteria are used to ensure that the nodes in a schema graph are all required.

During the process of change verification, a detected error needs to be fixed by modifying the schema graph, such as adding or removing nodes as well as adding or removing edges. Since all of the modification on the schema graph should to be verified, change verification may be trapped for repeatedly detecting and correcting. For example, a schema graph is checked to be correct with respect to criterion 5 and incorrect with respect to criterion 4. In this case, the graph will be modified to conform to criterion 4, which may result in violating other criteria. To avoid potential error, the graph needs to be re-examined with respect to other criteria. Moreover, verifying a change in an ad hoc way may cause the wrong deletion of a node. For example, a newly added node may be detected to be isolated. This will happen if its composition with other nodes does not be specified by the owner. When this structural incorrectness is detected, the node will be removed, which is semantically wrong. Therefore, the process of verification needs to be carefully designed. First, it should ensure that the each criterion should be checked only one time. Put differently, once an error is detected, the process of fixing this error should not violate the criteria that have been checked before. Second, it should ensure that the modification on the schema will not delete a node by error.

From the above analysis, the process of verifying changes will start at examining the semantic correctness. Once an error is detected, the schema graph will be modified to fix the error. This will ensure that the modification on a LCS schema graph at this step is for the semantic purpose. After that, it will examine the structural correctness. We will elaborate the process of change verification as below, where the details of change verification order is given.

Algorithm 8 Checking Data Transfers in a Schema Graph

1: Functional check_Data_Transfer($\mathcal{M}, N_c$)
Require: a LCS schema $\mathcal{M}$ and a set of nodes that are affected by the change N_c
Ensure: an updated $\mathcal{M}$
2: **for all** $n \in \mathcal{M}.DG.N$ **do**
3:     generating $n.mi$ and $n.mo$;
4: **end for**
5: $N_E = \phi$
6: **for all** $n \in N_c$ **do**
7:     $I_G = \cup_{i=1}^{n} n.mi_i.D$;
8:     **if** $(I_G \supseteq n.I)$==false **then**
9:         $N_E \leftarrow n$;
10:         $n.L = n.I - I_G$;
11:     **end if**
12: **end for**
13: **for all** $n \in N_E$ **do**
14:     **for all** $n' \in \mathcal{M}.DG.N$ and $n \neq n'$ **do**
15:         **if** n depends on n' with data D and $D \supseteq n.L$ **then**
16:             $\mathcal{M}.DG.DE \leftarrow (n', n, D)$; update $n.mi$ and $n'.mo$;
17:             $n.L = n.L - D$;
18:         **end if**
19:         **if** $n.L == \phi$ **then**
20:             $N_E = N_E - n$; break;
21:         **end if**
22:     **end for**
23: **end for**
24: **for all** $n \in N_E$ **do**
25:     **if** $n' \in \mathcal{M}.DG.N$ and $n'.O \cap n.L$ **then**
26:         $\mathcal{M}.DG.DE \leftarrow (n', n, n'.O \cap n.L)$; update $n.mi$ and $n'.mo$;
27:         $n.L = n.L - n'.O \cap n.L$
28:     **end if**
29:     **if** $n.L \neq \phi$ **then**
30:         $\mathcal{M}.DG.DE \leftarrow (n_e, n, n.L)$; updating $n.mi$ and $n_e.mo$;
31:     **end if**
32: **end for**

5.1.3.2 Semantic Verification

Semantic verification is to check whether a schema graph is correct using the two semantic correctness criteria. The criteria measure the correctness of both the data transfers and invocation order among services, which are embodied by the two edge sets in the schema graph: DE and CE. It is worth to note that the invocation order is determined by the data transfer. Therefore, we will first check the correctness of data transfer among services. Once an error is detected, it will be fixed by adding or removing edges in DE. After examining the data transfer, we will use the edges in DE to check the correctness of invocation order among services.

The first step of checking data transfers in a schema graph is to ensure that each service can get all the input it requires. It is to enforce the correctness criterion 4. This process is described in Algorithm 8. Our algorithm only checks the nodes that have been involved in the change. These nodes can be the newly added one or the nodes whose incoming and outgoing messages in DE have been modified, either by removing a data transfer, or removing a node. We use N_c to denote of a set of such nodes. There are two user nodes in the graph: n_ϵ and n_ω. n_ϵ only has outgoing messages containing the data provided by a LCS's users. n_ω only has incoming messages containing the data required by a LCS's users. Therefore, the user node n_ϵ n_ω may also be included in N_c if the user input or LCS output is required to be changed. For example, a travel agency LCS may want to provide the local map information to its users. In this case, n_ω will be included in N_c since its output changes. We first check whether the nodes in N_c can get all the required input. If not, these nodes will be added to a set N_E. The input that has not been covered by the node's incoming DE edges will be stored in $n.L$ (Line 6 to Line 12). The next step is to fix the errors by finding an alternative resource to supply the required input. The algorithm will follow three steps, which correspond to the three types of resources that a service node n can count on for their input. The resources include the service nodes that n has dependency relationship with, the users, and the other service nodes in the schema graph. The dependency relationship between different service nodes is defined in the proposed service ontology. It is described as a triplet, s_1, s_2, and D, meaning that s_1 depends on s_2 to provide D. Therefore, the algorithm will first check whether there are such nodes in the schema graph. If yes, the data transfer will be created and included in DE. $n.L$ will be updated, too. If $n.L$ is still not empty, the algorithm will find the service nodes in the schema graph that can provide the data left in $n.L$. It will compare between the output of other nodes in the graph and the data in $n.L$. If there is a match, the data transfer will be created and included in DE. If there are still some data items left in $n.L$, the algorithm will ask the user to provide the data. The reason that we put the user node as the last one to provide the data is based on an assumption. The assumption is that a LCS's owner will explicitly add a data transfer between the user node n_ϵ and the service node if he wants to let users provide the required information.

For each node in N_E, the algorithm needs to compare it's required input with the output of other nodes in the schema graph. Therefore, the maximum time complexity is $O(|N_E| * |\mathcal{M}.DG.N|)$.

Once the data transfer is verified, the consistency between the invocation order and the data transfer needs to be checked. This is for the purpose of ensuring that services can be orchestrated properly. As showed in Algorithm 9, for each edge m in DE, the algorithm will check whether there is a path in CE between $m's$ start node and $m's$ end node. If not, an edge pointing from the start node to the end node will be created and included in CE. This is to ensure that the invocation order between these two nodes is consistent with their data transfer. The path information can be stored and maintained by using a matrix.

Algorithm 9 Checking the Consistency between DE and CE in a Schema Graph

---

1: Functional check_Message_Exchange($\mathcal{M}$)
Require: a LCS schema $\mathcal{M}$
Ensure: an updated $\mathcal{M}$
2: **for all** $m \in \mathcal{M}.DG.DE$ **do**
3:     **if** $Is\_a\_path(\mathcal{M}.DG.CE, m.start, m.end) == false$ **then**
4:         $\mathcal{M}.DG.CE \leftarrow$ (m.start, m.end, true);
5:     **end if**
6: **end for**

Since Algorithm 9 will check each edge in $\mathcal{M}.DG.DE$, the time complexity is $O(|\mathcal{M}.DG.DE|)$.

5.1.3.3 Structural Verification

Structural verification is to check whether a schema graph is correct using the three structural correctness criteria. According to the criteria, the following types of nodes need to be removed from the schema graph: isolate nodes, the nodes that do not have any incoming CE edges, and the nodes that do not have any outgoing DE edges. Once a node is removed, all of its edges in DE and CE will be removed, too. This will change the incoming and outgoing edges of the removed node's neighbors. Therefore, removing a node may trigger the removing of other nodes. To avoid repeatedly checking the incoming and outgoing nodes in the schema graph, we will examine the path instead. This process is described in Algorithm 10.

Algorithm 10 Checking structural correctness of a Schema Graph

---

1: Functional check_Structure_Correctness($\mathcal{M}$)
Require: a LCS schema $\mathcal{M}$
Ensure: an updated $\mathcal{M}$
2: **for all** $n \in \mathcal{M}.DG.N$ **do**
3:     **if** $Is\_a\_path(\mathcal{M}.DG.DE, n, n_\omega) == false$ **then**
4:         $delete\_nodes(\mathcal{M}.DG, n)$;
5:     **end if**
6:     **if** $Is\_a\_path(\mathcal{M}.DG.DE, n_\epsilon, n) == false$ **then**
7:         $delete\_nodes(\mathcal{M}.DG, n)$;
8:     **end if**
9: **end for**

Algorithm 10 examines each node in the schema graph for one time. Therefore, the time complexity is $O(|\mathcal{M}.DG.N|)$.

Figure 5.2 shows the schema graph of the travel agency LCS after implementing the change in our running example. The Taxi service has been removed. All of its incoming and outgoing edges have been removed, too. The red nodes represent the newly added services, including Car Rental, Local Activities, and Traffic services. The red edges represent the newly added data

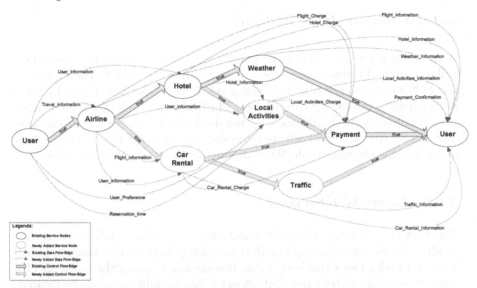

Fig. 5.2 The updated travel agency LCS schema

transfers and invocation orders. The red data flow edges will be generated first. For a Local Activities service, it requires three inputs: location information, user preferences and user information. The three data transfer edges need to be automatically generated so that the Local Activities service can get its required input. According to our algorithm, the dependency relationship will be first examined. We assume that a dependency relationship between the Local Activities and Hotel services is defined in the travel ontology. When these two services are combined together, the Hotel service will provide the location information. In this case, an edge pointing from the Hotel service to the Local Activities service will be generated. For the user information required by the Local Activities, our algorithm will check the output of other member services. Since the Airline has an output of flight information, which contains the user information that can be used by the Local Activities. Therefore, an edge pointing from the Airline service to the Local Activities service will be generated. The user preference cannot be provided by other services. In this case, the algorithm will explicitly require users to provide the information. An edge pointing from the user to the Local Activities will be generated. The generated edges will be included in the DE. After updating the data transferring, the invocation orders will be specified. For example, since there is a data transfer from the Airline service to the Local Activities service, a CE edge connecting these two services will be generated.

5.1.4 Compile LCS Instances

A LCS schema graph defines the participant services in the LCS and their collaboration. Therefore, once there is any update on a LCS schema graph, the LCS's instance needs to be recompiled. It may take two steps which are determined by the change requirement. The first step is to locate Web services that fulfill both the functional and non-functional requirement of changes. The second step is to orchestrate these services following their collaboration defined in the schema graph. We elaborate on these two steps as follows.

5.1.4.1 Locate Web Services

The first step of compiling a LCS instance is to locate Web services that fulfill both the functional and nonfunctional requirement of a change. It will be taken under two situations. First, if a change requires the addition of a functionality, the Web service that offers the functionality needs to be located. This could be the result of implementing the following change operators: $\triangle^S$ $(s, \mathcal{M}, op)$ and $\triangle^{S \leftrightarrow} (s_{old}, s_{new})$. Second, if a change is associated with a non-functional requirement, such as a context constraint or a quality requirement, the Web service that can fulfill the requirement needs to be located. This could be the result of implementing the following change operators: $\triangle^{CM}$ $(\lambda, \mathcal{M})$ and $\triangle^{QM} (\delta, \mathcal{M})$.

Our proposed service ontology classifies Web services into different categories based on their functionality. Each service node in a service ontology defines a type of functionality. A Web service subscribes to a service node if it provides the functionality. Therefore, the subscription relationship can be used to locate a Web service that fulfills a specified functional requirement.

The change operator $\triangle^{CM}$ $(\lambda, \mathcal{M})$ enforces a context constraint λ to a LCS defined by $\mathcal{M}$. Recall that λ is a triplet that consists of S, e, and v, where S is a set of outsourced abstract service of a LCS, e specifies the context type, and v specifies the new value of the context. Implementing this change operator follows two steps. First, it needs to perform a functionality-based Web service search. We specify an abstract service using the service node in a service ontology. Therefore, an abstract service is associated with a set of concrete Web services, which will be targeted during this step. Second, the services that fulfill the context constraint will be selected. This same steps are followed to implement the change operator $\triangle^{QM} (\delta, \mathcal{M})$.

5.1.4.2 Orchestrate Web Services

After locating services, the services that participate in a LCS can be determined. We use WS to denote these services. The services are expected to fulfill both the functional and non-functional requirements introduced by a change. The next step is to orchestrate them together. The orchestration of Web services follows the combination pattern defined in the LCS schema graph. An executable BPEL description of the service orchestration will be generated.

The two major components of a BPEL description are partners and activities. We will specify each service in WS as a *partner link*, using tags of <portType>, <operation>, and <input>. The directed edges in DE in a LCS schema graph correspond to the two types of BPEL activities: *receive* and *reply*. The directed edges of a LCS schema graph can be mapped to the different types of BPEL activities, including *receive, reply, sequence, switch, invoke, while*, etc. For example, the preparation of the required input messages for participant services can be specified using <assign> and <copy> tags. The parallelization of services can be specified using <invoke>. The conditional selection of services can be specified using <switch>, <case>, and <otherwise>.

5.2 Change Optimization

Due to the competition of service providers with similar functionalities, the updated LCS schema may result in multiple instantiations (we call them as *LCS instances*). Each of these instances satisfies the functional requirement specified by the change specification. However, they are differentiated from each other with respect to their non-functional properties, i.e, the quality of the provided service. We propose to optimize the LCS instance selection through quality assessment of all the LCS instances. Since providers may not always deliver according to their "promised" quality, relying only on provider promises may produce sub-optimal results. We use the *reputation* of concrete services in each LCS instance as an indicator of the services' past performances, i.e., their ability to "deliver," in accordance with the "promises" made about the Quality of Web service (QoWS). As depicted in Figure 5.3, we propose a two-phase optimization approach relying on the QoWS and reputation as the two criteria for providing the best LCS instance resulted from the change management process. We first use service reputation to filter out the services that have the low reputations. We then use QoWS as the second filter to choose the best one from the remaining trustworthy services. In what follows, we present the details of the two-phase change management optimization process.

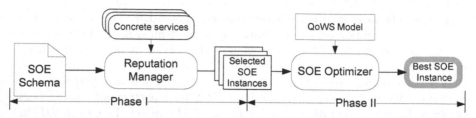

Fig. 5.3 Two-phase optimization process

5.2.1 Phase I: Reputation Based Optimization

The first optimization phase is to assess the reputation of the candidate Web services in a LCS instance. The result of this process is the list of Web services that have the high reputation. Since Web services are independent and autonomous, it is hard to have a central monitoring mechanism to assess their reputations. To address this issue, we use a *Reputation Manager* to assess the reputation of a concrete service involved in the LCS instance being evaluated. The reputation manager may inquire several peer *Reputation Managers*, and aggregate the respective personal evaluations for a service s_j. We assume a reputation collection model presented in [81], and extend it to the Web services domain using methods presented in [64]. The single derived value (obtained as a result of the aggregation of personal evaluations collected) is defined as the service provider's *aggregated reputation* in that *Reputation Manager*'s view. The LCS optimizer uses these aggregated reputation values for all the candidate services and filter out the ones that have the low reputation. Different *Reputation Managers* may employ different aggregation techniques. Therefore, the aggregated reputation value for the same provider may be different for each consumer, i.e., it may not be consistent across all consumers. Formally, the reputation of s_j, as viewed by a consumer i is defined as:

$$Reputation(s_j, i) = \bigwedge_{x \in L} (PerEval_k^{xj}) \tag{5.1}$$

where L denotes the set of service raters, k represents the different QoWS attributes (as reliability, availability, etc.), and $\bigwedge$ represents the aggregation function. It can be as simple as representing the union of personal evaluations where the output is a real number, or an elaborate process that considers a number of factors to assess a fairly accurate reputation value. Equation 5.1 provides an approximation of how the service reputation may be calculated. In the following, we build upon this equation to define key metrics for accurate reputation assessment. We aim to counter attacks related to deception in reputation management, i.e., identifying, preventing, and detecting malicious behavior of peers or a set of colluding peers acting as either service providers or raters. Specifically, we focus on the problems of *unfair ratings* through collusion (ballot stuffing or bad-mouthing). Problems as free riding, fake identities, ratings incentives, are outside the scope of this book.

Credibility of Raters: A major drawback of feedback-based systems is that all ratings are assumed to be honest and unbiased. However, in the real world we clearly distinguish between the testimonies of our sources and weigh the "trusted" ones more than others [48]. A Web service that provides satisfactory service, may get incorrect or false ratings from different raters due to several malicious motives. In order to cater for such "bad-mouthing" or collusion possibilities, a reputation management system should weigh the ratings of highly credible raters more than consumers with low credibilities [48, 97]. In our model, reputation is calculated as a weighted average according to the credibilities of the raters. Thus, Equation 5.1 becomes:

$$Reputation(s_j, i) = \frac{\sum_{t_x=1}^{L} (PerEval_k^{xj} * C_r(t_x, i))}{\sum_{t_x=1}^{L} C_r(t_x, i)} \quad (5.2)$$

where $Reputation(s_j, i)$ is the aggregate reputation of s_j as calculated by the service consumer i and $C_r(t_x, i)$ is the credibility of the service rater t_x as viewed by the service consumer i.

Personalized Preferences: Service consumers may vary in their reputation evaluations due to their differences in QoWS attribute preferences over which a Web service is evaluated. For instance, some service consumers may label Web services with high reliability as more reputable while others may consider low-priced services as more reputable. We allow the service consumers to calculate the reputation scores of the Web services according to their own *personal preferences*. Each service consumer stores its QoWS attribute preferences in a *reputation significance vector* (RSV). This allows the consumers the ability to weigh the different attributes according to their own preferences. Let $\phi_k^x(s_j, u)$ denote the rating assigned to attribute k by the service rater x for service provider s_j in transaction u, m denote the total number of attributes and RSV_{i_k} denote the preference of service consumer i for attribute k. Then, the local reputation for s_j as reported by service rater x (using i's attribute preferences) is defined as:

$$PerEval^{xj} = \frac{\sum_{k=1}^{m} (\phi_k^x(s_j, u) * RSV_{i_k})}{\sum_{k=1}^{m} RSV_{i_k}} \quad (5.3)$$

Reputation Fading: There are situations where all the past reputation data is of little or no importance. For instance, a Web service performing inconsistently in the past may ameliorate its behavior. Alternatively, a service's performance may degrade over time. It may be the case that considering all historical data may provide incorrect reputation scores. In order to counter such discrepancies, we incorporate temporal sensitivity in our proposed model. The rating submissions are "time-stamped" to assign more weight to *recent* observations and less to *older* ones. This is termed as *reputation fading* where older perceptions gradually *fade* and fresh ones take their place. We adjust the value of the ratings as:

$$PerEval^{xj} = PerEval^{xj} * f_d \quad f_d \in [0, 1] \qquad (5.4)$$

where $PerEval^{xj}$ is as defined above and f_d is the reputation fader. In our model, the recent most rating has the fader value 1 while older observations are decremented at equal intervals for each time instance passed. When $f_d = 0$, the consumer's rating is not considered as it is outdated. The "instance of time" is an *assigned* factor, which could be anywhere from a single transaction, ten transactions or even more than that. All transactions that are grouped in *one* instance of time are assigned the same fader value. In this way, the service consumer can define its own 'temporal sensitivity degree.' For example, a service can omit the fader value's effect altogether by assigning it a null value. We propose to use a fader value that can then be calculated as: $f_d = \frac{1}{P_u}$, where P_u is the total number of past transactions over which the reputation is to be evaluated. This allows the fader value to include all prior transaction history. However, as mentioned earlier, other calculated values for the fader are also acceptable. Incorporating the defined metrics together, the equation for overall reputation calculation becomes:

$$Reputation(s_j, i) = \frac{\sum_{t_x=1}^{L} \left[\frac{\sum_{k=1}^{m} (\phi_k^x (s_j, u) * RSV_{i_k})}{\sum_{k=1}^{m} RSV_{i_k}} * f_d * C_r(t_x, i) \right]}{\sum_{t_x=1}^{L} C_r(t_x, i)} \qquad (5.5)$$

Through experimental evidence we have found that the above equation provides a comprehensive assessment of the reputation of a given service provider.

Till now, the reputation manager comprehensively, efficiently assesses the service reputations, which enables the service optimizer to choose the Web services that have the high reputation. Considering the expected high volume of the available Web services on the Web, the result of composing these Web service would still be multiple LCS instances. Therefore, we will use the next phase to further optimize the result of the change management.

5.2.2 Phase II: QoWS Based Optimization

The reputation-based optimization helps select the concrete services with desired trustworthiness. This ensures the confidence on the consistency between the promised quality and the delivered quality of the selected services. In this section, we continue to present the QoWS based optimization that selects the best LCS instance.

We define a score function to compare the quality of LCS instances [100]. Since a LCS instance contains multiple operations, we need to aggregate the QoWS parameters from different operations. Table 3.1 lists the aggregate function for each of these QoWS parameters. Since users may have preferences over how their queries are answered, they may specify the relative importance of *QoWS* parameters. We assign *weights*, ranging from 0 to 1, to each *QoWS* parameter to reflect the level of importance. Default values are otherwise used.

We use the following score function F to evaluate the quality of the LCS instances. By using the score function, the optimization process is to find the LCS instance with the maximum score.

$$F = (\sum_{Q_i \in neg} W_i \times \frac{Q_i^{max} - Q_i}{Q_i^{max} - Q_i^{min}} + \sum_{Q_i \in pos} W_i \times \frac{Q_i - Q_i^{min}}{Q_i^{max} - Q_i^{min}})$$

where *neg* and *pos* are the sets of negative and positive *QoWS* respectively. In negative (resp. positive) parameters, the higher (resp. lower) the value, the worse is the quality. W_i are weights assigned by users to each parameter. Q_i is the value of the ith *QoWS* of the LCS instance obtained through the aggregate functions from Table 3.1. Q_i^{max} is the maximum value for the ith *QoWS* parameter for all potential LCS instances and Q_i^{min} is the minimum. These two values can be computed by considering the operations from service instances with the highest and lowest values for the ith *QoWS*.

By using the score function, the optimization process is to find the LCS instance that maximizes the value of F. We present two approaches for finding the best LCS instance: *exhaustive* search and *greedy* search.

The exhaustive search enumerates the entire space of LCS instances. Suppose that a LCS instance needs to access M Web services. We also assume that there are N competing service providers in each service. Therefore, the complexity of the exhaustive search is N^M, which is exponential.

The greedy search achieves the polynomial complexity by using a *divide-and-conquer* strategy. It generates an *optimal sub-LCS-instance* from each service through local search. It then combines these sub-LCS-instances to form the final LCS instance. In order to apply the divide-and-conquer strategy, we take logarithms on the aggregation functions for reliability and availability. Specifically,

$$Reliability = \sum_{i=1}^{n} log(rel(op_i)) \tag{5.6}$$

$$Availability = \sum_{i=1}^{n} log(avail(op_i)) \tag{5.7}$$

These enable to express the score of the final LCS instance as a linear combination of the scores from the sub-LCS-instances. Thus, the greedy search has a complexity of $N \times M$.

Chapter 6
Bottom-up Change Specification and Change Model

Modeling changes offers sufficient formalization required by change management in LCSs. Changes have been modeled using various tools and technologies [82]. For example, the Z language has been used to reflect changes in database schema [33]. However, changes to Web services are fundamentally different from changes in databases. Web services consist of behavioral aspects that are not relevant to data. In this chapter, we first propose a taxonomy of bottom-up changes. This allows us to define specific strategies to be applied to different types of changes. Based on the taxonomy, we then propose a formal model of bottom-up changes.

6.1 Change Specification

Our bottom-up approach for managing changes is highly dependent on the services that compose the LCS. Therefore, it is necessary to first define the changes that occur to Web services, and then map them onto the business level. In this chapter, we describe the types of changes that are present in LCS. We then define the concept of *service centric* dimensions of these changes. We categorize the types of service centric changes that must be managed in LCSs. These changes include *triggering* changes that occur at the service level and *reactive* changes that are executed at the business level. Finally, we provide rules for mapping triggering changes to their respective reactive changes.

6.1.1 Taxonomy of Changes

We distinguish between service and business layer changes as *triggering* and *reactive* changes, respectively. A triggering bottom-up change occurs at the service level, such as a change to service availability. A reactive change occurs at the business level in response to the triggering change, such as the selection of an alternative service. In this section, we define a taxonomy of bottom-up changes that we consider in a LCS. We first describe the triggering changes, followed by the reactive changes. Finally, we present a mapping between these two changes.

6.1.1.1 Triggering Changes

In our work, we assume that triggering changes occur asynchronously. For instance, the AA airline service may not change its data types while the triggering change of unavailability is being managed. Another assumption we make is that the service is associated with a set of states. We associate each change with a transition between two states: *precondition* and *postcondition*. For example, a precondition for AA's unavailability is that it was previously available and the postcondition is that it has become unavailable. Triggering changes and their respective preconditions and postconditions will later be used to model changes using Petri nets.

Our classification of triggering changes is derived from the perspective of a single member service. Let us take the example of AA's operation being unavailable. The operation may become unavailable because of request overload, rename, etc. In this case, we declare that the entire AA service is unavailable. We also assume that the inverse condition holds. For example, if AA becomes unavailable because of a network failure, we assume that all of its operations are also unavailable. Furthermore, we assume that services that trigger changes are *simple* services. In this book, we do not consider changes triggered by composite services. Recall that our focus in this book is on explicit bottom-up changes. Therefore, we do not taxonomize cascading or implicit bottom up changes. For example HZ car rental service may change its input parameter and require an airline code from the airline service. In this case, AA will need to change its output parameters to comply with HZ. We do not identify these types of changes in our work. Based on these assumptions, we divide triggering changes into two broad categories: *non-functional* and *functional* (Figure 6.1).

Non-Functional Changes

Non-functional changes represent the dependability, usability, and trust associated with a member service. This information may be stored by a third party, the LCS, or member services. We assume the information is stored as attributes that are maintained by an independent third party service provider. Changes to the trustworthiness of a Web service relate to the *security*, *reputation*, and *privacy* of a Web service. Changes in usability are

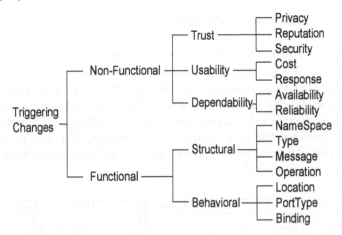

Fig. 6.1 Taxonomy of Triggering Changes

dependent on the *responsiveness* and service *cost*. Finally, changes to dependability are associated with the *availability* and *reliability* of the Web service. Changes to service dependability are binary, because they represent two distinct states. For example, a service may either be available or unavailable. Alternatively, changes to service trust and usability are non-binary. For instance, service cost may assume more than two values during a member service's lifetime. Therefore, we assume that a *threshold* is set and maintained by the LCS. This threshold declares the minimum and maximum intervals of a value accepted by the LCS. For example, the travel agency LCS has the threshold of minimum \$5 and maximum \$10 for any airline service cost. Every time a change occurs to the cost of a member AA service, it is compared with the threshold. Only if the change exceeds the threshold, we consider that a triggering change has occurred.

In the following sections, we consider non-functional changes to a member service, which is denoted by $\mathcal{M}$. Note that the changes we have defined, such as changes to availability, are applicable to member services only. Once a member service is replaced, it is no longer part of the change management mechanism. For example, the airline member service AA may become unavailable, and prompt the travel agency LCS to select an alternate airline service BA. After some time, AA may become available. However, since it is no longer a part of the travel agency LCS, the travel agency LCS does not manage the change in AA. Table 6.1.1.1 summarizes the non-functional changes in Web services.

Changes to Service Dependability

Availability is the probability that $\mathcal{M}$ is accessible. It is measured by the expression $\frac{UpTime(\mathcal{M})}{TotalTime(\mathcal{M})}$, where UpTime($\mathcal{M}$) is the time $\mathcal{M}$ was accessible for the duration of the measurement, TotalTime($\mathcal{M}$). $\mathcal{M}$ may become unavailable *during* or *prior to* LCS orchestration. This unavailability can be caused by network, server, or other failures. For example, the server hosting the **AA** service may go down before or during service consumption. The precondition for *changeAvailability* is that the service is available and the postcondition is that it becomes unavailable:

Change	Attribute	δ	Pre	Post
changeAvailability	WS_A	δ_A	WS_A	WS'_A
changeReliability	WS_L	δ_L	WS_L	WS'_L
changePrivacy	WS_P	δ_P	WS_P	WS'_P
changeSecurity	WS_S	δ_S	WS_S	WS'_S
changeReputation	WS_N	δ_N	WS_N	WS'_N
changeCost	WS_C	δ_C	WS_C	WS'_C
changeResponsiveness	WS_R	δ_R	WS_R	WS'_R

Table 6.1 Summary of Non-Functional Changes

- *Available:* A service is assumed to be available when a LCS is composed. Hence, availability is the initial state of a Web service. The availability of a service is expected to change throughout the execution of the LCS. For example, when the **AA** service is selected, it is assumed to be available. However, it may become unavailable during its consumption.
- *Unavailable:* During the orchestration of the LCS, a service or its required operations may become unavailable. This unavailability may be permanent or temporary. A service may become unavailable *during, before,* or *after* execution. This unavailability may be caused by network, server, or other failures. For example, the server offering the **AA** service may go down before or during the consumption of the service.

The *reliability* of $\mathcal{M}$ is the ability of the service to be executed within the maximum expected time frame. Reliability is computed based on historical data about invocations of the operation using the expression $\frac{Success(\mathcal{M})}{Invoked(\mathcal{M})}$, where Success($\mathcal{M}$) is the number of times that the service has been successfully executed within maximum expected time frame and Invoked($\mathcal{M}$) is the total number of invocations. The precondition for *changeReliability* is that the service must be reliable and the postcondition is its becoming unreliable:

- *Reliable:* A service is assumed to be reliable when a LCS is composed. Hence, reliability is the initial state of a Web service. The reliability of a service is expected to change throughout the orchestration of the LCS.

For example, a service may start to decrease its reliability in the presence of increased service request.

- *Unreliable:* During the orchestration of the LCS, a service or its required operations may become unreliable. This unreliability may be permanent or temporary. A service may become unreliable *during, before,* or *after* its execution. This unreliability may be caused by increased load, faulty programming at the server side, etc. For example, the server offering the AA service may not respond to every invocation call it receives.

Changes to Service Trust

Privacy is defined as the confidentiality maintained by $\mathcal{M}$. The privacy attribute indicates which parties are authorized to access the service's input and output parameters. It is set to one if $\mathcal{M}$'s input and output parameters should not be divulged to external entities (i.e., other than the service provider). If the access of $\mathcal{M}$'s operational parameters is not restricted by confidentiality, it is set to zero. The precondition for *changePrivacy* is private and the postcondition is non-private:

- *Private:* A service is assumed to be private when a LCS is composed. This assumption may be based on a minimum level represented by Privacy(WS_i). For example, the travel agency LCS may only consider doing business that has the privacy attribute set to 1. Alternatively, the travel agency LCS may not place any privacy restrictions on its member services. In this case, Web services with both zero or one privacy ratings may qualify as being "privacy preserving."
- *Non-Private:* During the orchestration of the LCS, a service's privacy may decrease from 1 to 0. This decrease may be permanent or temporary, and may occur only if the travel agency LCS sets its privacy requirement to one. A service may not become non-Private if the travel agency LCS's requirement is set to zero, as going below that number is not possible in our privacy representation method.

The *security* attribute describes whether $\mathcal{M}$ is compliant with security requirements. Indeed, service providers collect, store, process, and share information about millions of users who have different preferences regarding the security of their information. We identify three properties related to security: *encryption, authentication,* and *non-repudiation. Encryption* is a boolean that indicates whether $\mathcal{M}$'s messages are encrypted during transmission between requesters and providers. *Authentication* is a boolean that states whether $\mathcal{M}$'s consumers (users and other services) are authenticated (e.g., through passwords or certificates). *Non-repudiation* is a boolean that specifies whether participants (consumers and providers) can deny requesting or delivering the service after the fact. The security attribute Security($\mathcal{M}$) has a range between zero and three. The precondition for *changeSecurity* is secure and the postcondition is unsecure:

- *Secure:* A service is assumed to be secure when a LCS is composed. This assumption may be based on a minimum level represented by the range Security(WS_i). For example, the travel agency LCS may consider a service with the Security(WS_i) attribute being 2 or above to be secure.
- *UnSecure:* During the orchestration of the LCS, a service's security may drop below the required threshold. This decrease may be permanent or temporary, and may occur *during, before,* or *after* its execution. This decrease causes the service to become unsecure.

The *reputation* of $\mathcal{M}$ is a measure of the service's trustworthiness. It refers to the perception that an entity has about another entity (e.g., intentions, norms). In our case, it mainly depends on user experiences on invoking $\mathcal{M}$. Users are given a range to rank Web services (e.g., between 1 and 10). The highest value refers to the best ranking. Users may have different opinions on the same service. The reputation of $\mathcal{M}$ is defined by the average ranking given by users to the service. Reputation is computed by the expression $\sum_{u=1}^{n} \frac{Ranking_u(\mathcal{M})}{n}$, where $Ranking_u$ is the ranking by user u and n is the number of the times $\mathcal{M}$ has been ranked. The precondition for *changeReputation* is reputable and the postcondition is non-reputable:

- *Reputable:* A service is assumed to have a positive reputation when a LCS is composed. However, over time the reputation of the service may decrease below the minimum level required by the LCS. Let us assume that the travel agency LCS requires an airline service to have a minimum reputation of 5. If the number decreases, i.e., the reputation gets worse, the service is considered to have a negative repuation. However, if the number increases above 5, the service is considered to be reputable, as it meets the LCS's minimum requirements.
- *Non-Reputable:* A positive reputation indicates that a service is trustworthy. A service is maintained as having a positive reputation as long as it meets a "minimum" rating. During the orchestration of the LCS, a service's reputation may fluctuate. A service may acquire negative reputation *during, before,* or *after* its execution.

Changes to Service Usability

The *cost* attribute gives the amount required to consume $\mathcal{M}$. We assume that the amount is represented in dollars, and the currency remains constant. Also, we assume that the method of calculating cost is absolute, i.e., the cost is represented in exact dollar amount and is not based on a percentage/commission of transaction. We determine the cost of a service based on the LCS requirements. If the cost of $\mathcal{M}$ increases beyond the LCS's threshold, we determine that the cost has changed. The precondition for *changeCost* is affordable and the postcondition is unaffordable:

- *Affordable:* A service is assumed to be affordable when a LCS is composed. However, the service provider may decide to change the cost of the Web service after it has been composed by a LCS. For example, the travel agency LCS may incorporate the AA Web service at a time when it's cost was 100 dollars. At a later stage, the airline service may decide reduce its cost to 50 dollars. In this case the Web service still remains affordable, as it is clearly in the travel agency LCS's range of cost.
- *Unaffordable:* During the orchestration of the LCS, a service may increase its cost. required operations may become expensive. For example, the travel agency LCS may incorporate the AA Web service at a time when it's cost was 100 dollars. At a later stage, the airline service may decide to double its cost. Depending on the requirement of the travel agency LCS, this cost may exceed the maximum cost acceptable by the travel agency LCS. If the travel agency LCS set the maximum cost to 100 dollars, then, clearly, the travel agency LCS must consider utilizing services of a cheaper airline service.

Responsiveness measures the expected delay in seconds between the instance when $\mathcal{M}$ is initiated and the instance when it sends the results. Time($\mathcal{M}$) is computed using the expression $\text{Time}_{process}(\mathcal{M}) + \text{Time}_{results}(\mathcal{M})$. This means that the response time includes the time to process a service ($\text{Time}_{process}$) and the time to transmit or receive the results ($\text{Time}_{results}$). If a service does not respond within a "reasonable" time, we assume that the service's responsiveness has changed. The precondition for *changeResponsiveness* is responsive and the postcondition is unresponsive:

- *Responsive:* A Web service remains responsive as long as it meets the minimum requirements of the LCS. For example, if the travel agency LCS's requirement for the airline service's responsiveness is five seconds, the AA service is expected to conform to this requirement. If the reposiveness increases, the service is still considered to be responsive.
- *Unresponsive:* During the orchestration of the LCS, a service may decrease its responsiveness. For example, as soon as the AA service increases it's response time to more than 30 seconds, it is considered as unresponsive.

Functional Changes

Unlike non-functional changes, which are based on attributes, functional changes deal with changes to a service's WSDL description [22]. We represent functional changes as a combined execution of a *remove* followed by an *add*. We further classify functional changes into structural and behavioral changes (Figure 6.1). Structural changes refer to the operational aspects of

a Web service. For example, a structural change in an airline service can be
caused by changing the operations offered to a consumer. Changes to the
behavior of a Web service are indicated by changing its interaction with external entities. Functional changes to a member Web service occur when its
WSDL description is modified. We assume these changes are initiated by the
service provider. Table 6.1.1.1 gives a summary of functional changes to a $\mathcal{M}$
and are defined in the next sections.

Changes to Service Structure

The *structure* of a Web service includes high-level syntactic description of
a Web service that defines its name, URI, and other necessary information
to access the Web service. It is used to syntactically identify a Web service.
We identify the following change types that are necessary for determining
structural changes.

Change	Attribute	δ	Pre	Post
removeNameSpace	WS_N	$\delta^-{}_N$	WS_N	$WS^-{}_N$
addNameSpace	WS_N	$\delta^+{}_N$	WS_N	$WS^+{}_N$
removeType	WS_T	$\delta^-{}_T$	WS_T	$WS^-{}_T$
addType	WS_T	$\delta^+{}_T$	WS_T	$WS^+{}_T$
removeMessage	WS_M	$\delta^-{}_M$	WS_M	$WS^-{}_M$
addMessage	WS_M	$\delta^+{}_M$	WS_M	$WS^+{}_M$
removeOperation	WS_O	$\delta^-{}_O$	WS_O	$WS^-{}_O$
addOperation	WS_O	$\delta^+{}_O$	WS_O	$WS^+{}_O$
removePortType	WS_P	$\delta^-{}_P$	WS_P	$WS^-{}_P$
addPortType	WS_P	$\delta^+{}_P$	WS_P	$WS^+{}_P$
removeBinding	WS_B	$\delta^-{}_B$	WS_B	$WS^-{}_B$
addBinding	WS_B	$\delta^+{}_B$	WS_B	$WS^+{}_B$
removeLocation	WS_D	$\delta^-{}_D$	WS_D	$WS^-{}_D$
changeLocation	WS_D	$\delta^+{}_D$	WS_D	$WS^+{}_D$

Table 6.2 Summary of Functional Changes

The *namespace* attribute points to the URIs that support the preferred
namespaces that $\mathcal{M}$ will reference. Changes to namespace occur if a version
of existing framework is upgraded. For example, if the WSDL version is upgraded by $\mathcal{M}$'s service provider and a newer version needs to be utilized, the
LCS must update its interaction with $\mathcal{M}$ accordingly. At the time of orchestration, $\mathcal{M}$ is assumed to have a namespace. If a service discontinues support
for older versions of the namespace, it removes the namespace description in
its WSDL. The precondition for *changeNamespace* is the existing version of
the Namespace, WS_N. The postcondition is a new version of the Namespace
$WS^-{}_N$ and $WS^+{}_N$, for remove and add, respectively:

- $WS^+{}_N$: Over a period of time, the Web service provider may decide to add a namespace description to the existing description. This new namespace may reflect an upgrade in technology, or the use of variables from additional sources. The addition of a namespace results in a NamespaceAdded state.
- $WS^-{}_N$: A Web service provider may decide to remove a namespace. This change may be motivated by the need to discontinue supporting older versions of WSDL. For example, a service provide may add a namespace initially to upgrade the WSDL version. After all its consumers have upgraded to the newer version, the service provider can remove the older version.

Data types that are used by $\mathcal{M}$ in its messages and operations must be known prior to service invocation. This syntactic description of data types is required to provide an input to $\mathcal{M}$ and receive the output. A data type maybe removed or added from the list of service parameters at the service provider's discretion. The precondition for *changeDataType* is WS_T, which is the existing set of data types. The postconditions are $WS^-{}_T$ and $WS^+{}_T$:

- $WS^+{}_T$: During the orchestration of the LCS, a service may add to its data types. This change may be initiated by the service's requirement or mandated by regulation. For example, the airline service AA may add a numerical data type for accepting the customer's social security number.
- $WS^-{}_T$: A service may decide to remove a data type requirement. For example, AA may no longer require a customer's first name while executing the getFlightInfo operation.

Messages to and from $\mathcal{M}$ determine its structural model. Message are of four types: notification, request, response, and solicit response. The service provider may change the message type during $\mathcal{M}$'s lifecycle. The precondition for *changeMessage* is WS_M and the postconditions are for $WS^-{}_M$ and $WS^+{}_M$:

- $WS^+{}_M$: During the orchestration of the LCS, a service may add a required message. This change may be initiated by the service's requirement or mandated by regulation. For example, the airline service AA may add a notification message that presents the customer with a disclaimer.
- $WS^-{}_M$: A service may decide to remove a message requirement. For example, AA may remove the disclaimer notification message based on government regulations.

Messages are grouped together to form *operations*. These operations reflect the functionality provided by $\mathcal{M}$. $\mathcal{M}$ may change its functionality by changing operations. For example, the AA service may no longer offer an operation for making reservations. Instead, all reservations will be made through the "purchase ticket" operation. The precondition for *changeOperation* is WS_O and the postconditions are $WS^-{}_O$ and $WS^+{}_O$:

- $WS^+{}_O$: A service may add a required operation. This change may be initiated by the service's requirement or mandated by regulation. For example, the airline service AA may add an operation to solicit customer social security information.
- $WS^-{}_O$: A service may decide to remove an operation requirement. For example, AA may decide to discontinue providing flight timings to its customers.

Changes to Service Behavior

The behavior of a Web service describes how a service interacts with other entities in the LCS. This includes the communication protocols and the endpoints that are used for communication. We determine the following types that are necessary for determining behavioral changes.

Messages are exchanged through $\mathcal{M}$'s ports. The formats and ports associated with a message describe its interactions. $\mathcal{M}$ may add new ports for interaction, remove obsolete ports, or change existing ports. The precondition for *changePortType* is WS_P and the postconditions are $WS^-{}_P$ and $WS^+{}_P$:

- $WS^+{}_P$: Ports are the communication medium for Web services. A service may increase the number of ports that it offers for interaction. This increase may be based on an increased demand, addition to service functionality, or for scalability reasons.
- $WS^-{}_P$: A service may remove port descriptions from its WSDL. This removal may be initiated to prune inactive ports, to reduce the functionality provided by the service, or to improve performance of the service.

A *binding* determines the port and protocols through which $\mathcal{M}$ interacts. The precondition for *changeBinding* is WS_B and the postconditions are $WS^-{}_B$ and $WS^+{}_B$:

- $WS^+{}_B$: This postcondition represents the addition of binding information for the Web service. For example, the AA service may decide to offer binding via SMTP in addition to the HTTP binding.
- $WS^-{}_B$: A service may remove binding descriptions from its WSDL. This removal may be initiated for security and scalability reasons. For example, AA may have a robust security mechanism for the HTTP binding, but not for the SMTP protocol. Therefore, it may remove SMTP binding options.

The *location* is a high level description of $\mathcal{M}$. The precondition for *changeLocation* is WS_D and the postconditions are $WS^-{}_D$ and $WS^+{}_D$:

- $WS^-{}_D$: This postcondition represents the addition of location information for the Web service. For example, the AA service may decide to offer services from multiple locations.

- $WS^+{}_D$: A service may remove location descriptions from its WSDL. This removal may be initiated to reduce operating costs by eliminating or consolidating locations .

6.1.1.2 Reactive Changes

Each triggering change will initiate a reactive change at the business layer. Reactive changes may occur at the composition and orchestration levels of a LCS. For instance, a δ_T change in the AA service may trigger inconsistencies in the LCS composition, such as incorrect parameter data types. Alternatively, a δ_A change may disrupt LCS orchestration. We split the taxonomy of reactive changes into composition and orchestration (Figure 6.2). A third type of reactive change is referred to as *userAction*. We assume that each reaction may be overrided by the enterpreuer (or user). The user always has precedence over the *default* changes to the business layer, and may explicitly execute a reactive change. For example, if AA becomes unavailable, the user may decide to replace the service, or to execute the travel agency LCS without AA. We define composition and orchestration bottom up changes in our specification, since user level changes have been extensively discussed in the top down change chapters.

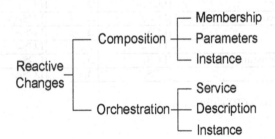

Fig. 6.2 Taxonomy of Reactive Changes

Composition Changes

We first define changes to LCS composition. Often a change such as δ_A will require the LCS to alter its composition. For example, the consistent unavailability of a marketing service may trigger the travel agency LCS to remove the service from its composition. We specify the following changes to LCS composition:

- **changeMember:** A changeMember consists of removeMember and/or addMember changes. Let us assume that the AA service becomes less responsive. In this case, the AA service will be removed and another Web service will be added to the LCS. However, if the newly added service also has a low response rate, both the new and the old airline services may be retained and the requests can be distributed between them.

- **changeParameter:**   Bottom-up changes may sometimes require more than just the removal and/or addition of Web services. For example, a change in AA's input/output data type may be managed by changing the parameters in the travel agency LCS's interface with AA. It is not necessary to replace the entire service based on this slight change. Therefore, this reconfiguration process updates the composition of a LCS to reflect changes in member services.

- **changeCompositionInstance:**   The order in which a LCS is composed may be changed. For example a triggering change of AA service unavailability may cause the travel agency LCS to orchestrate other services first. This change in order may override the current LCS composition temporarily or permanently, or exist in parallel with the original LCS specification.

Change	Attribute	Δ	Pre	Post
removeMember	LCS_M	Δ^-_M	LCS_M	LCS^-_M
addMember	LCS_M	Δ^+_M	LCS_M	LCS^+_M
removeParameter	LCS_P	Δ^-_P	LCS_P	LCS^-_P
addParameter	LCS_P	Δ^+_P	LCS_P	LCS^+_P
removeInstance	LCS_P	Δ^-_C	LCS_C	LCS^-_P
addInstance	LCS_C	Δ^+_C	LCS_C	LCS'_C
changeState	LCS_S	Δ_S	LCS_S	LCS'_S
changeServiceInstance	LCS_I	Δ_I	LCS_I	LCS'_I
changeOrder	LCS_O	Δ_O	LCS_O	LCS'_O

Table 6.3 Summary of Reactive Changes

Orchestration Changes

Unlike changes to LCS composition, orchestration changes deal with the LCS execution. For example, when the travel agency LCS is interrupted by a δ_A change in AA, it must suspend execution and react to the change. This may be accomplished by throwing and exception, compensating for the change with a LCS composition change of *changeMember*, and invoking the alternate service. The following changes occur to LCS orchestration:

- **changeState:**   Changes to LCS state are defined by the various stages of its execution. LCS execution has the following states: *halt*, *compensate*, *resume*, and *terminate*. Halt stops service execution in cases such as service unavailability. Compensate executes reactive changes in the LCS, such as selection of an alternate service. Resume restarts the LCS. Finally, terminate dissolves the LCS.

- **changeServiceInstance:** Changes to services may require the LCS to change the actual instances of member services. For example, following a change in availability, the travel agency LCS may change the instance of AA service and replace it with BA service.
- **changeOrder:** The order of service orchestration may be modified temporarily by a triggering change. For instance, if AA becomes unavailable, the travel agency LCS may change its execution order and invoke the hotel service before the airline service.

6.1.2 Mapping of Changes

A Mapping specifies how change instances in one layer corresponds to changes in another layer [86]. These mappings must remain consistant in the presence of frequent changes. When a change occurs at the service level, the business layer must react to manage the changes. Triggering changes have a reactive impact on the business layer of the LCS. In this section, we discuss the impact of δ changes to a LCS's business layer.

Changes in business layer are *sympatric* and translated with respect to the service layer changes. For example, a δ change in availability maps to a Δ change of changeInstance. Figure 6.3 maps each service level change to the corresponding business change. A dot at the intersection of service and business level changes indicates a relation between the δ and Δ changes. Each δ change is also mapped directly to *userAction*. In the next Section, we describe the rules for mapping triggering (δ) changes to reactive (Δ) changes.

6.1.2.1 Mapping Rules

Our approach of mapping changes is based on mapping rules. These rules are based on the triggering changes and their corresponding reactive changes. Some changes may have more than one rule associated with them. For example, if a Web service cost increases, the LCS may continue to use the service or decide to select an alternate service because the current service has become too expensive. Other changes may not cause any reaction. For example, if a Web service's cost decreases, the LCS will ignore this change, because it does not conflict with the service's goals. Still other changes may be ambiguous and require user interaction to be managed. An example is where a service may become available after a temporary unavailability. In this case, the Web service may again be integrated into the LCS, or the LCS may decide to continue using an alternate service. This decision is purely based on user discretion. Furthermore, the user has the option of overriding any of the rules.

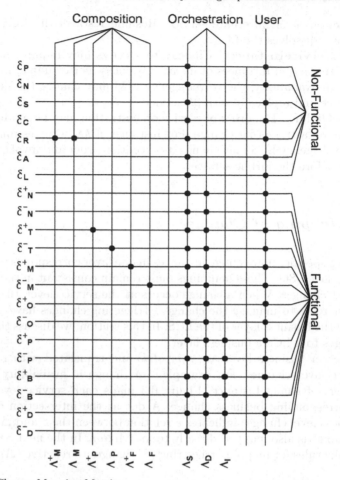

Fig. 6.3 Change Mapping Matrix

In this Section, we provide change mapping rules, where each rule is associated with a triggering change. We define the following rules for managing non-functional changes:

- **Rule 1:** If a *changeAvailability* change occurs, and the Web service is not executing, the LCS must remove this service and select an alternate service. If this change occurs while the LCS is executing, the LCS must wait for a bounded time, which may be defined by the user. If the service does not become available within that time, the LCS will select an alternate service and start execution of the alternate service. If this change occurs after the service is executed, the LCS will replace the service with an alternate service. If an alternate service does not exist, the LCS will be terminated. Alternatively, the user may override and continue the execution of the LCS without the unavailable Web service.

- **Rule 2:** If a service becomes unreliable, it may cause unexpected errors in LCS execution. If the service becomes unreliable before the execution of the LCS, it will be replaced by an alternate service. If the change occurs during LCS execution, the LCS will continue using the service and replace it after its execution. Finally, if the service becomes unreliable after execution of the LCS, it will be replaced by an alternate service. If an alternate service does not exist, the user must define whether to continue using the unreliable service or to terminate the LCS.

- **Rule 3:** The *changePrivacy* change will cause the LCS to abandon the service. We believe that privacy is an important criteria for selecting a service. If the service no longer qualifies the LCS's privacy requirements, it will be removed immediately from the LCS. This reaction is valid if the change occurs before, during, or after execution of the Web service.

- **Rule 4:** Similar to changes in service privacy, the *changeSecurity* change is very critical to the LCS. When this change occurs, the service is immediately removed from the LCS and an alternate service is selected. If no alternate service the LCS will be terminated or orchestrate without the unsecure service.

- **Rule 5:** If a *changeReputation* change occurs, the service will be immediately removed from the LCS composition. The reputation of the service describes its trustworthyness. Therefore, if the service is not trustworthy, the LCS must terminate all relationships with the service. The LCS will then select an alternate service, if one exists. If an alternate service does not exist, it will either terminate or execute without the service.

- **Rule 6:** If a *changeCost* change occurs, the Web service will be removed from the LCS composition, and an alternate service will be selected. This rule applies for a service before and after execution. However, if the service cost is increased during the execution, the LCS continues to use the service. Alternatively, the user may decide to continue using this service. For example, if an alternate service does not exist, or if the current service provides exceptionally good quality, the user can voluntarily decide to pay more for the current service instead of removing it from the current composition.

- **Rule 7:** If a *changeResponsiveness* change occurs before or after service execution, the unresponsive service will be replaced by an alternate service. If this change occurs during service execution, the LCS will continue to use the service and replace it after the execution is completed. However, in case of severe unresponsiveness or subsequent unavailability, the user may decide to stop using the service even if it is currently executing and choose an alternate service. This decision may be based on a certain allowable "threshold."

We define the following rules for managing functional changes:

- **Rule 8:** If a *addNamespace* change occurs, it is ignored because the previously existing Namespace is still valid. Therefore, it does not affect the execution of the Web service.
- **Rule 9:** If the *changeNamespace* change occurs, the new version of the Namespace is cashed within the LCS. The new Namespace is compared for its compliance with the LCS. Finally, the LCS is reconfigured to represent changes to the Namespace.
- **Rule 10:** If a *removeNamespace* change occurs, the LCS must re-cache the Web service description. Based on the new Namespace, the LCS must be reconfigured. If the LCS cannot be reconfigured, it must select an alternate service.
- **Rule 11:** If an *addType* change occurs, the LCS must be reconfigured to reflect the addition of the type. Consider the example where the airline service adds a required input parameter of telephone number. In this case, the LCS must modify its interaction with the Web service to support the required parameter.
- **Rule 12:** If a *changeType* change occurs, the LCS must be reconfigured to reflect the changes in the type. Consider the example where the airline service changes the type of telephone number from number to string. In this case, the LCS must modify its interaction with the Web service to support the required change in parameter type.
- **Rule 13:** If a *removeType* change occurs, the LCS must be reconfigured to reflect the removal of the type. Consider the example where the airline service removes a required input parameter of telephone number. In this case, the LCS must modify its interaction with the Web service to eliminate the use of the removed parameter.
- **Rule 14:** If an *addMessage* change occurs, the LCS must be reconfigured to incorporate the new message. Consider the example where the airline service adds a notification message if the reservation was successful. In this case, the LCS must modify its interaction with the Web service to accept the notification.
- **Rule 15:** If a *changeMessage* change occurs, the LCS must be reconfigured to reflect the changes in the message. For example, if the message includes new parameters, the LCS must deal with them appropriately.
- **Rule 16:** If a *removeMessage* change occurs, the LCS must be reconfigured to reflect the changes in the service messages. Consider the example where the airline service removes a notification message. In this case, the LCS must modify its interaction with the Web service so that it does not expect a notification message.
- **Rule 17:** If an *addOperation* change occurs, the LCS must be reconfigured to reflect the changes in the operation. Consider the example where the airline service adds a required operation for validating the user. In this case, the LCS must modify its interaction with the Web service to support the required validation.

- **Rule 18:** If a *changeOperation* change occurs, the LCS must be reconfigured to reflect the changes in the operation. For example, if the structure
  of the operation changes (i.e., the types of messages or parameters), the
  LCS must deal with them by changing its configuration.
- **Rule 19:** If a *removeOperation* change occurs, the LCS must be reconfigured to reflect the changes in the service operation. Consider the example
  where the airline service removes an operation being used by the LCS. In
  this case, the LCS must modify its interaction with the Web service so
  that it does not use the removed operation. Alternatively, the user may
  decide to select an alternate service, if the removed operation was critical
  to the functionality of the LCS.
- **Rule 20:** If an *addPortType* change occurs, the LCS must be reconfigured
  to reflect the changes in the operation. Consider the example where the
  airline service adds a required portType for certain service requestors. In
  this case, the LCS must modify its interaction with the Web service to
  interact through the new portType.
- **Rule 21:** If a *changePortType* change occurs, the LCS must be reconfigured to reflect the changes in the operation. For example, if the portType
  changes from HTTP to SMPT, the LCS must deal with them by changing
  its configuration.
- **Rule 22:** If a *removePortType* change occurs, the LCS must be reconfigured to reflect the changes in the service portType. Consider the example
  where the airline service removes a portType being used by the LCS. In
  this case, the LCS must modify its interaction with the Web service so
  that it does not use the portType. Alternatively, the user may decide to
  select an alternate service, if the removed portType was critical to the
  functionality of the LCS.
- **Rule 23:** If an *addBinding* change occurs, the LCS must be reconfigured
  to reflect the changes in the binding. Consider the example where the AA
  service adds a required binding for certain users. In this case, the LCS
  must modify its interaction with the Web service to support the required
  validation.
- **Rule 24:** If a *changeBinding* change occurs, the LCS must be reconfigured
  to reflect the changes in the operation. For example, if the structure of the
  operation changes (i.e., the types of messages or parameters), the LCS
  must deal with them by changing its configuration.
- **Rule 25:** If a *removeBinding* change occurs, the LCS must be reconfigured
  to reflect the changes in the service binding. Consider the example where
  the airline service removes an operation being used by the LCS. In this
  case, the LCS must modify its interaction with the Web service so that
  it does not use the removed operation. Alternatively, the user may decide
  to select an alternate service, if the removed operation was critical to the
  functionality of the LCS.
- **Rule 26:** If an *addLocation* change occurs, the LCS must be reconfigured
  to reflect the changes in the operation. Consider the example where the

airline service adds a required operation for validating the user. In this case, the LCS must modify its interaction with the Web service to support the required validation.

- **Rule 27:** If a *changeLocation* change occurs, the LCS must be reconfigured to reflect the changes in the operation. For example, if the structure of the operation changes (i.e., the types of messages or parameters), the LCS must deal with them by changing its configuration.
- **Rule 28:** If a *removeLocation* change occurs, the LCS must be reconfigured to reflect the changes in the service location. Consider the example where the airline service removes an operation being used by the LCS. In this case, the LCS must modify its interaction with the Web service so that it does not use the removed operation. Alternatively, the user may decide to select an alternate service, if the removed operation was critical to the functionality of the LCS.

We classify changes as critical and non-critical. *Critical* changes require immediate action. For example, if a service removes a required operation, the LCS must immediately replace the service. *Non-critical* changes can be managed once the LCS has orchestrated the concerned service. For example, if the cost of AA increases during its orchestration, the travel agency LCS may complete its orchestrate before managing the change. In this case, the travel agency LCS will select an alternate service when it needs to invoke an airline service again. In our work, we classify all non-functional changes except change in availability as non-critical changes. All functional changes and change in availability are classified as critical changes.

6.2 Change Model

Modeling provides a systematic means for managing a LCS. Models are used to accurately identify the types of changes that may occur in a LCS, and to verify that the changes have been managed effectively. In this chapter, we discuss the theoretical basis of our change modeling technique. In particular, we discuss Lewin's model and describe how it is applicable to modeling changes to service oriented LCSs. Lewin's model has been applied successfully in the past, and we describe how it forms a solid basis for modeling changes to LCSs. We then model triggering and reactive changes using Petri nets. Triggering changes are modeled using ordinary Petri nets. Reactive changes are modeled using reconfigurable Petri nets. Because of the complexity of changes in LCSs and their management, formal modeling is a useful method to improve the understanding of the problem and consequently the solution. Petri net theory provides algorithms and methods, which are directly applicable to the change modeling. Other modeling and specification techniques have been proposed, but lack easy formalization features required by change management [82, 33, 74, 45].

6.2.1 Lewin's Change Model

The work of Kurt Lewin dominated the theory and practice of change management for over forty years [14]. Lewin's most cited work is his contribution to organizational change referred to as the *3 step model*. This model describes the change process as: *unfreeze, moving,* and *refreeze* [14, 77]. *Unfreeze* refers to creating a motivation and readiness to change in an organization. Lewin describes that this step is initiated when an "equilibrium" of an organization is destabilized. *Moving* is the process of evaluating the change and determining the appropriate propagation mechanism. *Refreezing* is the final step in Lewin's three step model, which refers to integrating the change into the organization and resuming its orchestration. It consists of the actions an organization takes to regain its equilibrium. In our work, unfreeze refers to the detection of a triggering change in a LCS. Moving is the propagation of triggering changes. Refreeze is the reaction to the triggering change, and the subsequent *safe* state of the LCS.

Critics of Lewin point the limitation of his change model in the presence of organizational politics and conflicts. However, these issues do not affect the bottom-up management of changes in LCS. Our assumption is that bottom-up changes are not driven by political agenda. Another critical approach to change management states that changes cut across different functions, time periods, hierarchical divisions, without the "neat" starting or finishing points defined by Lewin. This *processual* approach declares change as an "untidy" and complex process in an organization [14]. One of the main focus of our work is to organize and define a clear taxonomy of bottom-up changes in LCSs, and make change management a neat and systematic process, which would enable the automation of change management. Therefore, the processual approach does not fit well into our current research. More recent approaches tend to take a holistic view of the organizations and their environments and challenge the notion of change as an ordered, rational, and linear process. There is an emphasis that change is heavily influenced by culture, power, and politics [14]. We define bottom up change management as an ordered process, and therefore, build on Kurt Lewin's three step model.

Definition 6.1: *Bottom Up Change Management.* Bottom up change management is the establishment of automated processes in a LCS that allow the LCS to dynamically adapt to changes in its environment. We follow Kurt Lewin's concept of homeostasis or *dynamic stability*, which establishes a set of states for a changing system [14]. We consider the occurrence and subsequent detection of a change as the destabilizing factor. When a change occurs, the LCS is no longer in an equilibrium. Moving requires the changes to be propagated in the system. Finally, refreeze is the reaction to the changes.

The states of a LCS are classified into a set of safe (ST_s) and unsafe (ST_u) states. When a LCS transitions from a *safe* to an *unsafe* state, it invokes the process of change management. Once the change is managed, the LCS moves into a safe state.

Definition 6.2: *Safe State* (ST_s). A state is safe if and only if: (i) the execution of a LCS has not been interrupted by a triggering change, or (ii) if a triggering change has occurred it is (a) documented in the taxonomy and (b) has been managed successfully. Every time a LCS moves from a safe to an unsafe state, a change has occurred. These changes are predefined in our taxonomy. A safe state ensures that the LCS is compliant with its member services. With reference to Lewin's model, a safe state is present before the unfreeze and after the refreeze steps. An example of a safe state is the state of the LCS when it is first composed. In this case, the execution of the LCS has not been interrupted by a change, and there are no pending changes to be managed.

Definition 6.3: *Unsafe State* (ST_u). A state is unsafe if it does not meet the requirements of a safe state. Specifically, an unsafe state is achieved if the (i) LCS has been interrupted by an undocumented change, or (ii) the LCS has been interrupted by a documented change, but change management has not been completed. An unsafe state indicates that the LCS is not in compliance with its member services. In this case, executing the LCS may result in unexpected or undesired results. Therefore, if the LCS enters this state, either the corresponding change must be managed, or the LCS must be terminated. In Lewin's model, this state occurs between the unfreeze and refreeze steps.

In broad terms, the changes of LCS states describes its behavior [46]. The notion of a state depends on the topic of research. For example, a state may be the (i) internal execution of an LCS's Web services, (ii) a "part" of the state that is relevant to the LCS, or (iii) the state of the external world from the LCS's perspective. These states are changes based on some *action*. This action may be represented by the (i) messages exchanged between Web services, (ii) activities within a Web service, or (iii) events in a LCS. We use all three to describe changes in Web service states. Each of this activity is grouped into a *change type*. In our work, Web service change types are represented by a safe/unsafe state pair. Examples of Web service states are available and unavailable. In this case, the available state is the safe state and unavailability results in an unsafe state. The LCS also has distinct states corresponding to the states of the member services. If a member service is not in a safe state, the LCS is also in an unsafe state. For example, if a service becomes unavailable, the LCS state is unsafe. This mapping of changes presents how Lewin's model fits in our approach of defining, modeling, and managing changes.

The goal of change management is to provide efficient automated methods of detection, propagation, and reaction to changes in the LCS environment.

When a change is successfully detected, it must be propagated to all entities that are affected by the change. Finally, the LCS must react to the change and transition towards a safe state. Essentially, we need a mechanism to maintain state of the LCS over a long period of time, without sharing it across multiple instances of the LCS. Also, we need to manage the metadata about the Web service instances in the LCS.

6.2.2 Petri Nets as a Modeling Tool

Petri nets have been used to model a variety of concurrent and discrete event distributed systems [58, 54, 40, 41, 43, 50]. We model changes using Petri nets because of their applicability to LCS modeling. The behavior of a LCS is described by the evolution of its Petri net model. As the Petri net evolves, the system attains different safe and unsafe states that can be completely defined by the marking of a Petri net model. For example, Petri nets readily model the states when the travel agency LCS is unsafe because of a triggering change, and the subsequent safe state achieved after managing the triggering change. Furthermore, Petri nets map directly to our change specification. Therefore, Petri nets preserves all the details of our change specification while modeling the changes accurately. For example, Petri nets can easily represent the safe an unsafe states of Web service and the LCS. They represent changes between these states as transitions. Furthermore, the use of reconfigurable Petri nets allows us to incorporate our mapping rules into the Petri net model. This allows us to completely model our change specification, without the need to use additional modeling tools.

6.2.2.1 Fundamentals of Petri Nets

A Petri net is a special type of graph. While many Petri nets are multigraphs, we consider only ordinary Petri nets for this brief introduction. In many applications, parallel edges are very useful and the multigraph properties of Petri nets can be used to an advantage. However, they introduce notational and other complexities that are best addressed when extensions to ordinary Petri nets are considered (e.g., colored Petri nets). A second characteristic of Petri nets as graphs is that they are bipartite graphs. This means that they have two types of nodes. Different symbols are used to distinguish the two types of nodes. By convention, the first type of node is called a *place* and is denoted by a circle or ellipse. The second type is called a *transition* and is denoted by a solid bar or a rectangle. The edges of a Petri net are called *arcs* and are always directed. Our representation of these symbols is shown in Figure 6.4. An edge can connect only two nodes that belong to different types (bipartite graph). Therefore, there can be an arc from a place to a transition,

Place   **Transition**   **Arc**

Fig. 6.4 Symbols Used to Denote Petri Net Entities

from a transition to a place, but not from a place to a place or a transition to a transition.

Definition 6.4: *Petri Net.* A Petri net *(PN)* is a bipartite directed graph represented by a quadruple $PN = (P, T, I, O)$ where:

- $P = \{p_1,...,p_n\}$ is a finite set of places
- $T = \{t_1,...,t_m\}$ is a finite set of transitions
- $I(p,t)$ is a mapping P × T corresponding to the set of directed arcs from places to transitions
- $O(t,p)$ is a mapping T × P corresponding to the set of directed arcs from transitions to places

Ordinary Petri nets consist of functions I and O that take the values of 0 or 1. Other types of Petri nets (e.g., fuzzy nets) may use values from a non-boolean or "fuzzy" set. An example of an ordinary Petri net is depicted in Figure 6.5, denoted by PN_1. Places are represented by circles and transitions by rectangles. This is the convention that will be adopted for Petri nets in our work. The quadruple that defines PN_1 is represented as follows:

$$P = \{P_1, P_2\}$$
$$T = \{T_1\}$$
$$I = \{P_1\}$$
$$O = \{P_2\}$$

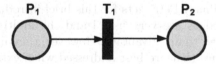

Fig. 6.5 Petri net PN_1

The set of all input places of a transition t are denoted by $\odot t$, also called the *preset* of t. $t\odot$ denotes the set of all output places of transition t, called the *postset* of t. Similarly, the preset for place p is denoted by $\odot p$, and its postset is denoted by $p\odot$. For the Petri net PN_1, the following relations hold:

$$\odot p_1 = \phi$$
$$t_2\odot = p_2$$

By defining the set of places, transitions, and the presets and postsets either of all places or of all transitions, we obtain an equivalent representation of the structure of a Petri net. The concepts of preset and postset become very useful in describing algorithms for the analysis of Petri nets. Furthermore, these presets and postsets are applicable in modeling preconditions and postconditions of service changes, respectively.

Definition 6.5: *Subnet.* A subnet of a Petri net PN = (P, T, I, O) is a Petri net $PN_s = (P_s, T_s, I_s, O_s)$ such that $P_s \subseteq P$ and $T_s \subseteq T$, and I_s and O_s are the restrictions of I and O to P × T and T × P, respectively.

Definition 6.6: *Path.* A path is a set of k nodes and *k-1* arcs, for some integer k, such that the i-th arc either connects the i-th node to the i+1-th node, or the i+1-th node to the i-th node. The path is directed, if for all i = 1, 2, ..., k, the i-th arc connects the i-th node to the i+1-th node. A path in which no arc is traversed more than once is called a *simple* path. A path in which no node is traversed more than once is an *elementary* path.

Petri nets would not be very useful, if all we could do is draw a diagram describing the relationships among the objects represented by the nodes. There are other established techniques to do this that are easy to use, and have supporting software. An essential feature of Petri nets is that they can be executed. One can observe the interactions between the components and study the dynamics of the system modeled by a Petri net. We introduce the marking of a Petri net and the firing of transitions. This will lead us to further characterization of the properties of ordinary Petri nets.

In addition to the two types of nodes (places and transitions) and the arcs, a fourth object is introduced to describe the dynamics of a Petri net. This object is the *token*, denoted by a solid dot •, and residing inside the circles representing the places. In ordinary Petri nets, the tokens do not represent specific information and are not distinguishable. They are only markers, indicating the presence or absence of whatever they represent (condition, signal, piece of data to be consumed, etc). Places can hold an arbitrary number of tokens, or they can be restricted as to the number they can hold (capacitated places). A simple arc from a place to a transition indicates that the transition requires one token in that place as one of the conditions for it to be enabled. In a multigraph, the multiplicity of the arc denotes the number of tokens from that place that the transition requires to be enabled. In this introduction, we will assume no restriction in the number of tokens a place may hold, and we will assume that the arc multiplicity is one.

Definition 6.7: *Marking.* A marking of a Petri net, denoted by *M*, is a mapping P × 0,1,2,..., which assigns a non-negative integer number of tokens to each place of the net. A marking can be represented by an *n*-dimensional integer vector whose components correspond to the places of the net.

The marking vector represents the state of the Petri net, i.e., the distribution of tokens in the places of the net defines its state. The service state changes when the distribution of tokens changes. It should be apparent that the number of states of a Petri net is usually very large. Consider, for example, a net in which the places are allowed to hold at most one token. If there are n places in the net, then the possible number of states of that Petri net is $2n$. The process by which the distribution of tokens changes is the *firing* of transitions.

Definition 6.8: *Firing.* A transition t is enabled by a given marking M if and only if there is at least one token in each input place of t. When a transition is enabled, it can fire. A token is removed from each of the input places of t (the preset of t) and a token is generated in each of the output places of t (the postset of t). The marking M of the Petri net is replaced by a new marking M'.

These definitions complete the required background on Petri nets. We use these basic definitions for Petri net modeling in our work. Several extensions to Petri nets have been described, which are described in the related work section.

In our work, we use ordinary Petri nets to model triggering changes. Each change is represented by a transition and the precondition and postconditions of the respective changes are represented by Petri net places. Reactive changes are modeled using Reconfigurable Petri nets. Transitions represent changes to the LCS, and places represent the pre and post conditions. For reactive changes to LCS composition, the places represent the state of the LCS composition. Places in the orchestration change Petri nets represent the state of the LCS orchestration.

6.2.3 Modeling Triggering Changes with Ordinary PNs

Ordinary Petri nets or *OPN* are a well-founded process modeling technique that have formal semantics. They have been used to model and analyze several types of processes including protocols, manufacturing systems, and business processes. Visual representations provide a high-level, yet precise language, which allows expression and reasoning about concepts at their natural level of abstraction. Services are basically a partially ordered set of changes. Therefore, it is a natural choice to map it into a Petri net. For instance, changes are modeled by transitions and the state of the service modeled by places. The arrows between places and transitions are used to specify causal

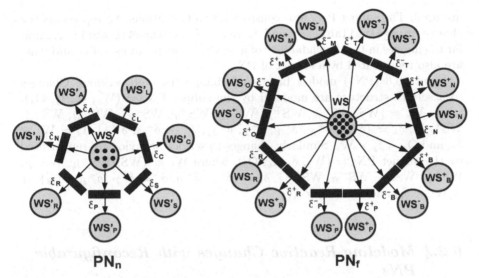

Fig. 6.6 Ordinary Petri Nets for Triggering Changes

relations between preconditions and postconditions.

Definition 6.9: $\mathcal{T}$-*Change.* $\mathcal{T}$-Change is a Petri net $\{W, \delta, S, i, o, l\}$, where:

- W is a finite set of places representing the states of a Web service
- δ is a finite set of transitions representing changes to Web service
- $S \subseteq (W \times \delta) \cup (\delta \times W)$ is a set of directed arcs representing a precondition and postcondition of changes in service state
- i is the input place, or starting state of the Web service
- o is the output place, or the ending state of the Web service

Figure 6.6 (PN_n) models non-functional changes to Web services. It consists of eight places and seven transitions. WS is the initial place of PN_n. It represents the initial state of the Web service (when the LCS is composed). WS consist of seven tokens, each representing one of the seven non-functional changes. Every time a change occurs, the corresponding token is fired. If more than one change occurs, the corresponding token for each change type is fired. For example, if a member service becomes unavailable, the transition δ_A will be enabled and the corresponding token will be fired.

The subnet representing dependability changes is $PN_d = (W_d, \delta_d, I_d, O_d)$, where $W_d = \{WS, WS'_L, WS'_A\}$, $\delta_d = \{\delta_A, \delta_L\}$, $I_d = W_d \times \delta_d$, and $O_d = \delta_d \times W_d$. The place WS indicates that the service is both available and reliable. It contains two tokens (one for availability and the other for reliability). WS'_A represents a service that has become unavailable. When a service becomes unavailable, the availability token is moved from WS to WS'_A. Similarly, WS'_L represents a service that has become unreliable, and the token is moved to WS'_L. If a service becomes both unreliable and unavailable, both the tokens are fired. The subnet PN_d also consists of two transitions. δ_A represents the change changeAvailability, and δ_R represents changeReliability. Similar to changes in the dependability of a service, changes to usability and trust are also represented by a subnet of PN_n.

Figure 6.6 (PN_f) models functional changes to Web services. Changes to a service structure are modeled by the subnet $PN_s = (W_s, \delta_s, I_s, O_s)$, where $W_s = \{WS, WS^-{}_N, WS^+{}_N, WS^-{}_T, WS^+{}_T, WS^-{}_M, WS^+{}_M, WS^-{}_O, WS^+{}_O,\}$, $\delta_s = \{\delta^-{}_N, \delta^+{}_N, \delta^-{}_T, \delta^+{}_T, \delta^-{}_M, \delta^+{}_M, \delta^-{}_O, \delta^+{}_O\}$, $I_s = W_s \times \delta_s$, and $O_s = \delta_s \times W_s$. Similarly, changes to service behavior are represented by the subnet $PN_b = (W_b, \delta_b, I_b, O_b)$, where $W_b = \{WS, WS^-{}_R, WS^+{}_R, WS^-{}_P, WS^+{}_P, WS^-{}_B, WS^+{}_B\}$, $\delta_b = \{\delta^-{}_R, \delta^+{}_R, \delta^-{}_P, \delta^+{}_P, \delta^-{}_B, \delta^+{}_B\}$, $I_b = W_b \times \delta_b$, and $O_b = \delta_b \times W_b$.

6.2.4 Modeling Reactive Changes with Reconfigurable PNs

A LCS can practically be modeled as a composition of Web services. This composition can be based on BPEL or another language. However, to maintain a generic and expressive model of a LCS, we use Petri nets to visualize the composition of Web services. We model each service as a place. The invocation of member services is represented by a Petri net transition. A transition also represents the return of control and data from the member service to the LCS. The execution of Web services can be modeled as a sequential, parallel, iterative, and conditional execution [40]. We assume that the execution of Web services in our LCS is sequential. For example, the travel agency LCS first invokes an AA service, receives the output, then invokes a HZ service, and so on.

We have surveyed several extensions of Petri nets for modeling reactive changes. However, they lack the ability to model dynamic changes. For example, a change in the configuration of the LCS is not readily modeled by a *colored* PN. *Reconfigurable* PNs provide a formalism for modeling these changes. They support internal and incremental description of changes over an external and uniform description. Therefore, this type of Petri net is a natural choice for modeling reactive changes. Reconfigurable petri nets are an extension of Petri nets and a subclass of net rewriting systems. They merge Petri nets with graph grammars and are best represented by Valk's Self-Modifying Nets [58]:

Definition 6.10: *Reconfigurable Petri net (RPN).* A reconfigurable Petri net is a structure $N = (P, T, R, \gamma_0)$, where $P = \{p_1,...,p_n\}$ is a nonempty and finite set of places, $T = \{t_1,...,t_m\}$ is a nonempty and finite set of transitions disjoint from $P(P \cap T = \emptyset)$, $R = \{r_1,...,r_h\}$ is a finite set of rewriting rules,

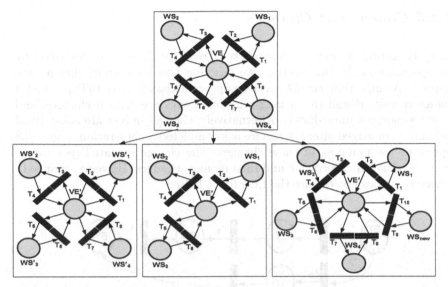

Fig. 6.7 RPN for Reactive Composition Changes

and γ_0 is the initial state.

Net rewriting systems have states represented by Petri nets. Arcs of Petri nets are either the (i) firing of a transition, or (ii) change of system configuration. While the firing of a transition is basic, and previously discussed, change in system configuration is more complex. Change in configuration is based on a (i) net rewriting rule $r \in R$, where $r = \{L, R, T, \bullet T, T \bullet\}$, and (ii) restriction $\Gamma = (P, T, F) \subseteq \Gamma' = (P', T', F')$ if $\Gamma \subseteq \Gamma_0'$ and $R_r \subseteq R_r'$. Using a RPN, we can model changes by representing a change in LCS orchestration via transitions, and a change in its composition using a rewriting rule.

We define γ_0 as the initial state when the LCS is composed, since change management will be initiated some time after the initial composition. Therefore, we say that the domain of γ_0 is LCS_0, or $DOM(\gamma_0) = LCS_0$, where LCS_0 is the initial state. In our scenario, we group the places LCS as LCS_U, LCS_V, and LCS_W. LCS_U is the set of places $\{LCS_1, LCS_2, LCS_3, LCS_4\}$, where U represents changeMember. LCS_V is the set of places $\{LCS_5, LCS_6, LCS_7, LCS_8\}$, where LCS_V represents changeParameter. LCS_W is the set of places $\{P_9, P_{10}, P_{11}, P_{12}\}$, where LCS_W is changeOrder. We distinguish the roles A, B, and C between transitions T. A is the set of transitions $\{T_1, T_2, T_3, T_4\}$, that indicate removal of a Web service, B is the set of transitions $\{T_5, T_6, T_7, T_8\}$ that indicate addition of a service, and C is the set of transitions $\{T_9, T_{10}, T_{11}, T_{12}\}$. Figure 6.7 presents an RPN representing changes to service composition. It presents the initial state of the LCS (top), change in service composition (left), removal of service (center), and addition of service (right).

6.2.5 Concurrent Changes

Every triggering change corresponds to a reactive change, as described by our specification. In this Section, we describe how concurrent changes are mapped. Assume that the AA service triggers a change in dataTypes and a change in cost. Recall that changes in dataTypes are critical changes, and must be managed immediately. Alternatively, changes in cost are non-critical and may be managed after the service has completed orchestration. Figure 6.8 represents the mapping of these changes. The change in dataTypes causes the LCS to halt orchestration and then manage changes. However, change to service cost does not require the LCS to be halted.

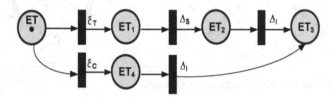

Fig. 6.8 Petri Net Representing Concurrent Changes

Change	Petri Net
δ^-_N	[0 1 0 0 0 0 0 0 0 0 0 0 0 0 0 0 0 0 0 0 0]
δ^+_N	[0 0 1 0 0 0 0 0 0 0 0 0 0 0 0 0 0 0 0 0 0]
δ^-_T	[0 0 0 1 0 0 0 0 0 0 0 0 0 0 0 0 0 0 0 0 0]
δ^+_T	[0 0 0 0 1 0 0 0 0 0 0 0 0 0 0 0 0 0 0 0 0]
δ^-_M	[0 0 0 0 0 1 0 0 0 0 0 0 0 0 0 0 0 0 0 0 0]
δ^+_M	[0 0 0 0 0 0 1 0 0 0 0 0 0 0 0 0 0 0 0 0 0]
δ^-_O	[0 0 0 0 0 0 0 1 0 0 0 0 0 0 0 0 0 0 0 0 0]
δ^+_O	[0 0 0 0 0 0 0 0 1 0 0 0 0 0 0 0 0 0 0 0 0]
δ^-_P	[0 0 0 0 0 0 0 0 0 1 0 0 0 0 0 0 0 0 0 0 0]
δ^+_P	[0 0 0 0 0 0 0 0 0 0 1 0 0 0 0 0 0 0 0 0 0]
δ^-_B	[0 0 0 0 0 0 0 0 0 0 0 1 0 0 0 0 0 0 0 0 0]
δ^+_B	[0 0 0 0 0 0 0 0 0 0 0 0 1 0 0 0 0 0 0 0 0]
δ^-_D	[0 0 0 0 0 0 0 0 0 0 0 0 0 1 0 0 0 0 0 0 0]
δ^+_D	[0 0 0 0 0 0 0 0 0 0 0 0 0 0 1 0 0 0 0 0 0]
δ_A	[0 0 0 0 0 0 0 0 0 0 0 0 0 0 0 1 0 0 0 0 0]
δ_L	[0 0 0 0 0 0 0 0 0 0 0 0 0 0 0 0 1 0 0 0 0]
δ_P	[0 0 0 0 0 0 0 0 0 0 0 0 0 0 0 0 0 1 0 0 0]
δ_R	[0 0 0 0 0 0 0 0 0 0 0 0 0 0 0 0 0 0 1 0 0]
δ_N	[0 0 0 0 0 0 0 0 0 0 0 0 0 0 0 0 0 0 0 1 0 0]
δ_C	[0 0 0 0 0 0 0 0 0 0 0 0 0 0 0 0 0 0 0 0 1 0]
δ_S	[0 0 0 0 0 0 0 0 0 0 0 0 0 0 0 0 0 0 0 0 0 1]

Table 6.4 Triggering Petri Nets

6.2.6 Petri Net Representation

The Petri Net Markup Language (*PNML*) is a proposal of an XML-based
interchange format for Petri nets. Originally, the PNML was intended to
serve as a file format for the Java version of the Petri Net Kernel, but it
turned out that currently several other groups are developing an XML-based
interchange format too. Therefore, the PNML is only one contribution to
the ongoing discussion and to the standardization efforts of an XML-based
format. The specific feature of the PNML is its openness: It distinguishes
between general features of all types of Petri nets and specific features of a
specific Petri net type. The specific features are defined in a separate Petri
Net Type Definition (*PNTD*) for each Petri net type. Furthermore, several
specific features are used in more than only one Petri net type. Therefore,
there is a Conventions Document containing specific Petri net features. Thus,
a concrete PNTD adds its its type specific features to PNML by referring to
the Conventions Document. The standardization efforts have mainly an effect
on this Conventions Document [8].

Petri Nets are traditionally represented as an incidence matrix. $\mathcal{M}$ is a i
$\times$ j matrix whose j columns correspond to the transitions and whose i rows
correspond to the places of the net. $\mathcal{M}$ is generated by using the following
equation:

$$\mathcal{M}_{ij} = \text{output}(t_j, p_i) - \text{input}(p_i, t_j) \text{ for } 1 < i < n, 1 < j < m.$$

Since there are no self-loops in the triggering Petri net, we may safely
create this matrix. Note that self loops in a Petri net cancel each other to yield
a zero in the matrix, thus losing track of the existence of the self-loop. Since
the Petri nets defined for changes are *sparce*, we have compressed them and
use arrays as a representation. We define the Petri nets that represent each
functional and non-functional triggering changes in Table 6.4. The reactive
Petri net generated by the LCS agent is present in Table 6.5.

Change	Petri Net
Δ^-_M	[0 1 0 0 0 0 0 0 0 0]
Δ^+_M	[0 0 1 0 0 0 0 0 0 0]
Δ^-_P	[0 0 0 1 0 0 0 0 0 0]
Δ^+_P	[0 0 0 0 1 0 0 0 0 0]
Δ^-_C	[0 0 0 0 0 1 0 0 0 0]
Δ^+_C	[0 0 0 0 0 0 1 0 0 0]
Δ_S	[0 0 0 0 0 0 0 1 0 0]
Δ_I	[0 0 0 0 0 0 0 0 1 0]
Δ_O	[0 0 0 0 0 0 0 0 0 1]

Table 6.5 Reactive Petri Nets

Chapter 7
Bottom-up Change Management

One of the most important requirements for managing changes is to guarantee consistency and correctness of a LCS in the presence of frequent changes. The LCS is likely to undergo significant functional and non-functional changes during its lifetime. Therefore, it is necessary for the LCS to automatically check for and safeguard its consistency. In this chapter, we present an approach to automatic management of bottom-up changes using Petri nets. The automatic management of changes is slated to play a major role in service oriented enterprises and LCS. Bottom up change management requires a systematic approach that is specifically defined and executed automatically. We use our Petri net change specification as the basis for managing changes in a LCS. We divide the process of change management into three distinct steps: *detection, propagation,* and *reaction*(Figure 7).

After the bottom up change specification is defined, we initiate the automatic management of the LCS. Detecting the respective changes is the first step of change management. All changes identified in the triggering changes taxonomy are subject to detection. Detection involves a service agent that monitors the member Web service. Each change type has an associated set of rules for detection. For example, an airline service may change its input parameters. When this change occurs, the LCS must detect the change using some predefined detection rules. We define these detection rules in the first step of our change management policy.

Communicating changes in the LCS is necessary for managing changes. Each change that is successfully detected by the service agent must be promptly and accurately communicated to the LCS agent. We take the example where a service agent detects a change in service parameters. Recall that this change requires the LCS to modify its composition. For the LCS to effectively change its composition based on the new parameters, the service agent must communicate the changes to the LCS agent. The most effective method of communication between two distributed entities is defined by a communication protocol. We define this communication protocol as the second step in managing changes.

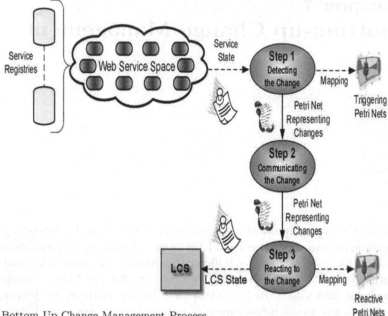

Fig. 7.1 Bottom Up Change Management Process

Every change that is communicated to the LCS agent initiates a reactive process. This process is based on a set of reaction rules, which consume the information communicated from the service agents. The reaction rules specify the course of action for the LCS to manage the change. For example, assume that the marketing service increases its price. The LCS agent derives that this specific increase in price is not acceptable to the LCS, and therefore, reacts to the change. The reaction to this change can be to select an alternate marketing service or to orchestrate the travel LCS without any marketing service.

7.1 Detecting Triggering Changes

Change detection is the awareness that a change has occurred and the subsequent identification of its cause. Our approach to detecting changes is based on using agents that play the role of *monitors* and *notifiers* [60, 6]. These agents are Web services that monitor the participant Web services for relevant changes (e.g. functional and non-functional) and notify LCS agents about the change. Change may be detected by a periodic *pull* or *push* [68]. In a periodic push, the Web service itself propagates changes to the service agents in regular intervals, sometimes in large batches. Alternatively periodic pulling requires that the service agents accesses remote Web services periodically to read current descriptions and update local replicas as necessary. One motivation for performing periodic pushing is that one-way messages can be used in place of more expensive, round-trip ones. Also, services can control the amount of local resources devoted to replica synchronization. Periodic pulling, on the other hand, has the advantage that services are not required to be active participants in the replica synchronization protocol. Instead, they need only respond to description read requests from the LCS, a standard operation in most environments.

We assume that changes to Web services are detected through a *push-based* strategy using soft states [72]. *Soft states* is a method used to maintain membership of entities in a loosely coupled system, such as the LCS. This method requires that a member service periodically send "refresh" messages to renew its membership. These messages are sent to a node that maintains the membership information. In our case, the provider Web services are members or participants in the LCS. The membership information is stored in the LCS *schema*. LCS agents act as intermediaries between the schema and the service agents. They are also responsible for the maintenance of the schema by updating it at the time of change. A participating Web service is assigned to each service agent that monitors changes in the status of that service. This agent periodically verifies the state of the service and its operations [30]. To verify changes in the state of a service, the agent will send "alive" messages to the Web service within a *chronon*. A chronon is the the minimum granularity of time for our system [35]. Let us assume that for our example, the chronon is set to the duration between invocation of two consecutive Web services. If the Web service responds, it is assumed to be alive and its state is updated in the schema. However, if a response message is not received from the Web service within an acceptable time limit, the service is considered as unavailable. Any change to a service description (e.g., rename or change of parameters) implies that the change was made explicitly by the Web service programmers. This justifies our assumption that the Web service description in the UDDI and Semantic registries will be appropriately updated after an operation change. We assume that these changes will further be propagated to the service agents. To detect changes in the description of a Web service, we implement one of the various algorithms available [19, 25].

7.1.1 Push Based Detection Techniques

In this section, we survey of selected push based change detection methods. The first major push based detection we discuss is *RSS* feeds or *Really Simple Syndication*. It is a way of keeping automatically aware of Web site updates. The way people find Web sites, blogs, and other content they like on the net is changing. While the majority still seek out sites of interest through search engines and keep addresses bookmarked, others increasingly use RSS. It delivers content to people that is of interest to them. Millions of news, Weblogs, and ordinary Web sites carry RSS feeds which alert people when a site has been updated [80]. Internet service providers and web portals, like *BT Yahoo*, have leveraged its potential and have made RSS an integral part of how the portals work.

We use a similar approach to pushing changes to service agents. We assume that all changes that a service agent is concerned with are pushed to it by an RSS feed by the service provider.

WS-Event is a research effort by *HP* to introduce a publish/subscribe framework for event notification [32]. It is a part of HP's *Web Service Management Framework*. An *event* is a change in the state of a resource or request for processing. We assume that each event is from the domain of changes we have specified. An event *producer* is an entity which generates notifications. In our case, this would be the member Web service. An event *consumer* is a receiver of notifications. The service agent represents the event consumer in our LCS model. A *notification* is an XML element representing an event. One or more notifications are emitted by an event producer and received or retrieved by one or more event consumers. To achieve scalability, WS-Event uses a subscription mechanism by which an service agent informs the member service that it is interested in receiving notifications. Subscriptions allow the service to plan and allocate resources depending on the number of subscribers, event notification types and access modes and length of subscriptions. Subscriptions have a limited duration in time. For instance, it might last for an hour. This ensures that if the LCS was dissolved without cancelling its subscription, resources would not be held indefinitely and recovered by the member service. Subscription can be renewed before it expires.

WS-Eventing is a standard proposed by BEA, *CA*, IBM, Microsoft, Sun, and TIBCO [11]. This specification defines a protocol for one Web service (called an "event sink") to register interest (called a "subscription") with another Web service (called an "event source") in receiving messages about events (called "notifications"). We use this standard for detecting triggering changes. WS-Eventing provides a push-based delivery of notifications. We assume that the event notification sends the updated version of the changed attribute. For example, if the *AA* service's operation has changed, the notification will consist of the type of change (Operation) and the updated attribute (new operation signature).

7.1.2 Petri Net Mapping Rule for Detection

We use the Petri net based model of changes to represent the detection of triggering changes. The changes are detected at the service layer and represented as a matrix at the ontology layer. We identify the following rules for detecting functional and non-functional changes. If a non-functional attribute is updated, the existing and updated values are compared. For example, if the cost attribute is updated, we compare both the values. If the updated value is greater than the threshold for that value, we identify the change in cost. If the value is less, we ignore the change. For the functional changes, we compare the WSDL description of Web services. If the WSDL description of a Web service is modified, the existing and updated descriptions are compared. For example, if the operation is updated, we compare both the operational descriptions. In this case, the number of input/output parameters may be different, the operation name may have changed, or the operation may no longer be offered by the service. Once changes have been detected by the service agent, we define the rules for mapping the changes onto a Petri net. These rules may be defined in plain text, or represented by a formal language, such as the Rule Markup Language (*RuleML*) or Extensible Rule Markup Language (*XRML*) [49]. We use the former to define the following mapping rule for change detection:

Rule 1: Map the current service state as a set of precondition places in the triggering Petri net. Map the updated service state as the set of postcondition places in the triggering Petri net. Compare the values precondition and postcondition places of the Petri net. If there is a difference between any precondition and postcondition place, we place a token in the respective precondition place. This token will enable the change transition.

Consider the example where the AA service changes its availability, while all other attributes remain constant. This change may be cause by AA's scheduled maintenance. In this case, we map the change onto the non-functional Petri net (Figure 7.2). The figure consists of one token that represents change in the service availability. This enables transition δ_A, while all other transi-

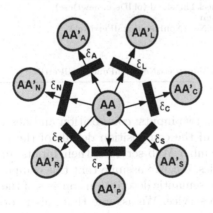

Fig. 7.2 Non-functional Petri Net for AA

	δ_A	δ_N	δ_R	δ_P	δ_S	δ_C	δ_L
AA'$_A$	1	0	0	0	0	0	0
AA'$_N$	0	0	0	0	0	0	0
AA'$_R$	0	0	0	0	0	0	0
AA'$_P$	0	0	0	0	0	0	0
AA'$_S$	0	0	0	0	0	0	0
AA'$_C$	0	0	0	0	0	0	0
AA'$_L$	0	0	0	0	0	0	0
AA	-1	0	0	0	0	0	0

Table 7.1 Matrix for AA Non-functional Changes

tions are disabled. This Petri net indicates the detection of a δ_A change in
AA.

We define the matrix in Table 7.1.2 for representing the Petri net for AA,
where j = { δ_L, δ_A, δ_N, δ_R, δ_P, δ_S, δ_C} and i = {WS, WS'$_L$, WS'$_A$, WS'$_N$,
WS'$_R$, WS'$_P$, WS'$_S$, WS'$_C$}. The Matrix will be generated by the service
agent responsible for monitoring the AA service.

7.1.3 Detection Algorithm

Algorithm 11 Change Detection Algorithm

```
1:  ChangeDetection (Input: oldDesc, newDesc)
2:  while newDesc do
3:      Compare (oldDesc[Functional], newDesc[Functional])
4:      if oldDesc[Functional] ≠ newDesc[Functional] then
5:          GeneratePetriNet (FunctionalPetriNet)
6:      end if
7:      Compare (oldDesc[NonFunctional], newDesc[NonFunctional])
8:      if oldDesc[NonFunctional] ≠ newDesc[NonFunctional] then
9:          Threshold = CheckThreshold (oldDesc, newDesc)
10:         if Threshold then
11:             GeneratePetriNet (NonFunctionalPetriNet)
12:         end if
13:     end if
14: end while
15: ChangeReaction (FunctionalPetriNet, NonFunctionalPetriNet)
```

Algorithm 11 takes two inputs: composition and description. The composition input consists of the composition details of the LCS. For example, it
consists of all the member Web services, their inputs and outputs, relationship with other entities, etc. We assume that this composition information is
defined in BPEL. The semantic description consists of the ontological markup
for the member Web service. We assume that this information is presented
in OWL-S. For detection purposes, we only utilize the extensible list of at-

tributes defining non-functional properties of a Web service. Finally, the syntactic description of a service is presented in a WSDL format. The detection algorithm continuously checks for triggering changes. It initiates a loop for checking semantic and syntactic descriptions of each Web service. This loop is executed for each member service extracted from the composition. When a change is detected, the algorithm generates an incidence matrix for the Web service.

7.2 Propagating Changes

Change propagation is required when a change in one Web service affects other entities in the LCS. In this case, all affected parties must be informed of the changes. All these changes must be managed before the LCS can arrive at a safe state. We consider two methods of change propagation in our work: *strict* and *lazy*. Strict propagation uses a *brute-force* method of conveying changes to the CA_e. For example, changes to a Web service description may be immediately propagated to CA_e by CA_s. This implies that every change that occurs in the Web service will cause the service agent to propagate the changes before the Web service is orchestrated. If the LCS finds that the service has changed, it will dump the contents of its local schema and refresh it using the latest information from the service provider. This can have some very significant performance implications, ethe domain of changesally when the service resides on a distant network. Therefore, this method of propagation should be used only when it is absolutely necessary that the service being orchestrated is always up-to-date at the time its invokation. It also tends to completely defeat the local caching done by the LCS if there are several updates taking place concurrently on member services. Strict change propagation does not guarantee that the member service is in its most current form. It only indicates that the next time the service is executed, the LCS will see the latest description. In our approach, we do not perform polling or background operations to constantly propagate changes. We only perform propagation when the LCS must execute the service.

7.2.1 Lazy Propagation of Changes

Lazy change propagation is the default policy and is the most desirable in terms of efficiency and performance. Lazy change propagation works by only propagating changes when the LCS cannot locate the desired Web service. At this point, the LCS must physically recache the service data. Eventually, the LCS will dump its cache and retry the orchestration that it was in the process of executing when it found that the service had changed. We assume that the LCS can cache a fairly large amount of service data for that meets its requirements. This policy tends to be very efficient and will provide the best performance overall. However, it does leave the job of requesting change propagation up to the LCS agent. The amount of memory used for buffering service data can affect how often the LCS agent requests change propagation using lazy change propagation.

We use a publish-subscribe mechanism to propagate changes in the system. For example, the LCS composition contains references to all member services that are composed into the LCS (i.e. that are part of the system). LCS agents update the composition in case of any change. The update involves the removal of the service reference stored in the composition. Since a service reference must be present in the composition before it can be invoked, the removal of service reference terminates the membership of that service.

7.2.2 Propagation Algorithm

Typically, technical specifications for the Web specify a language or a protocol. A protocol is a language for messages, plus a set of constraints on the sequence of messages. A language is a set of symbols, the syntactic constraints on the way they are combined, and the semantics of what they mean at a certain level [7]. We define the *Change Agent Protocol* (*CAP*) for communication between the service and LCS agents. The CAP defines the message sent by or on behalf of a service agent to an LCS agent. The service agent is identified by $\mathcal{CA}_s$, and the LCS agent is identified by $\mathcal{CA}_e$.

CAP presents an asynchronous form of communication between $\mathcal{CA}_s$ and $\mathcal{CA}_e$. The following is an overview of the communication process. $\mathcal{CA}_s$ detects a change in the associated Web service. It identifies the type of change and communicates the appropriate Petri net to $\mathcal{CA}_e$ through a publish/subscribe method. Upon receiving the information from $\mathcal{CA}_s$, $\mathcal{CA}_e$ determines the reaction that must be taken to manage the change occurring at the Web service. $\mathcal{CA}_s$ may send messages to $\mathcal{CA}_e$ as often as a change occurs, and is not required to wait for the previous message to be processed by $\mathcal{CA}_e$. This constitutes an asynchronous form of communication between the two change agents. Each change is detected by $\mathcal{CA}_s$ based on our change management model. These changes are propagated to $\mathcal{CA}_e$. $\mathcal{CA}_e$ determines the course of action to manage the change at $\mathcal{CA}_s$ based on the change rules.

7.3 Reacting to Triggering Changes

In this section, we define how we execute reactive changes based on the information propagated by the service agents. First, the LCS agent receives a matrix indicating the change that has occurred. It then maps the triggering change to the appropriate reactive change. We use our mapping matrix for this conversion. Finally, the reactive change is executed by the LCS agent. We consider the following types of reactive changes:

- **RemoveMember:** A Web service is removed from the LCS by making its operations unavailable to the LCS. For example, if a Web service becomes permanently unavailable, it is removed from the LCS composition. A remove partner operation followed by an add partner operation constitutes a "replace" or "change" partner operation.
- **AddMember:** Services are added into the LCS when their need is determined by the entrepreneur. A service is added in the initial composition of the LCS, and if a change occurs in a Web service. For example, the AA airline service may become less responsive. In this case, another Web service may be added to the LCS to replace the existing service. However, if the newly added service also has a low response rate, both the new and the old airline services may be retained and the requests can be distributed between them.

  - **SelectPartner:** Whenever a need for a service is determine (e.g., adding a service), the select operation identifies the required Web service. After this service is selected, it is added to the LCS.
  - **ComposeLCS:** The operations of the newly added Web service are plugged into the LCS. For example, if an airline service is added, the reservation and purchase ticket operations are integrated into the travel LCS.

- **changeOrchestration:** Often bottom-up changes require more than just the removal and/or addition of Web services. For example, a change in the Web service's input data type may be managed by reconfiguring the LCS input/output parameters. It is not necessary to replace the entire service based on this slight change. Therefore, the reconfigure operation updates its composition to reflect changes in member Web services.

  - **RecacheDescription:** If a service description changes, it must be reflected in the LCS composition. This will ensure successful orchestration of a member service.
  - **RemovePartner:** A Web service is removed from the LCS by making its operations unavailable to the LCS. For example, if a Web service becomes permanently unavailable, it is removed from the LCS composition. A remove partner operation followed by an add partner operation constitutes a "replace" or "change" partner operation.
  - **ComposeLCS:** The operations of the newly cashed service description are plugged into the LCS. For example, if an airline service is added, the reservation and purchase ticket operations are integrated into the travel LCS.

- **changeOrchestration:** When a LCS is interrupted by a stimulating change, it must change its execution phase to react to the change. For example, if a member service becomes unavailable, the LCS must pause it's execution by declaring a fault, compensate the change by selecting an alternate service, and invoke the alternate service.

  - **Fault:** If a service is not required for the LCS, the LCS may continue its orchestration. For example, if the AA service state changes from available to unavailable, the service is frozen but the LCS remains operational. However, if a critical service becomes unavailable, the LCS orchestration must be temporarily paused.
  - **Compensate:** After a change has been detected and a fault executed, the LCS can proceed with performing a compensation function. This compensation function involves either a composition or orchestration change.
  - **Invoke:** A paused LCS is resumed by the unfreeze operation. For example, if an alternate service is selected to replace an unavailable service, the LCS is immediately resumed.
  - **Terminate:** If an LCS is unable to function because of missing critical services, the LCS is terminated or dissolved.

Reaction to change depends on the (i) type of change and (ii) availability of alternate services. In case of a functional change, an alternate service must be selected to fulfill the user request. The service selection stage is initiated and provided with the description of the required service. At this point, the quick and dynamic discovery of alternate services is crucial to the successful execution of the LCS. If an appropriate service does not exist (or cannot be located), the user request must be canceled. However, if an alternate service is selected successfully, it is registered with the participant list and request processing is resumed. In the event of an internal service level change (e.g. change in stock prices), the previous data must be replaced with the current response. In the following sections, we first describe the details of selecting an alternate service. We then present the algorithm for maintaining consistency in the data returned by a Web service.

The problem of discovering and selecting the Web services necessary to construct LCS can be addressed by leveraging the semantic support proposed in Chapter 2. The Web service space identified by an ontology may consist of more than one service that satisfies the LCS goal. From the LCS point of view, a community may consist of several *candidate* services.

Definition 7.2: *Candidate Service.* A candidate service is a Web service that is capable of providing the services required by a LCS but is not currently a part of the LCS. It may also be referred to as an *alternate* service.

Formally, a Web service is a candidate service WS_c such that (i) $WS_c \subset \{WS_t\}$ and (ii) $WS_c \Rightarrow goal(LCS)$ where "$\Rightarrow$" represents "satisfies" and "goal(LCS)" is the goal of the LCS determined by the entrepreneur. In other words, a candidate service can be selected and integrated by an LCS in order to fulfill its goals. However, the LCS selects a *single* service out of these candidate services. We refer to this service as the *primary* service.

Definition 7.3: *Primary Service.* A primary service is the *optimal* service for the LCS among all the available candidate Web services and is chosen to be part of the LCS.

A primary service is, thus, a Web service WS_p such that (i) $WS_p \subset \{WS_c\}$ and (ii) $|WS_p| = 1$.

If an alternate service cannot be selected from *any* community, the LCS must abort all requests and terminate its services. Dissolution of a LCS will require the LCS to be "unregistered" from all service registries. Any pending or executing requests will be cancelled. Finally, all *implicit* and *explicit* obligations of the LCS will be dissolved.

Algorithm 12 Change Reaction Algorithm

1: **ChangeReaction (Input:** FunctionalPetriNet, NonFunctionalPetriNet)
2: ReactivePetriNet = ϕ
3: **while** FunctionalPetriNet **do**
4:    ReactivePetriNet = Map (FunctionalPetriNet, ReactivePetriNet)
5: **end while**
6: **while** (NonFunctionalPetriNet) **do**
7:    ReactivePetriNet = Map (NonFunctionalPetriNet, ReactivePetriNet)
8: **end while**
9: **while** (NonFunctionalPetriNet) **do**
10:    **if** (ReactivePetriNet) **then**
11:       Execute (ReactivePetriNet)
12:    **end if**
13: **end while**

7.4 Change Management Algorithm

In this section, we propose the algorithm for managing bottom-up changes. As depicted in the algorithm 13, the algorithm has two input parameters: executionTime and LCS concrete service list. executionTime is the time required to orchestrate a LCS. It stays positive for the LCS lifetime. LCS concrete service list refers to the list of all Web services that are currently participating in the system.

Algorithm 13 Change Management Algorithm

```
 1: ChangeManagement (Input: executionTime, LCS concrete service list)
 2: time = executionTime
 3: while time != 0 do
 4:    for all each Web Service WS_i in LCS concrete service list do
 5:        send alive message to WS_i
 6:        if not alive then
 7:            remove WS_i from LCS concrete service list
 8:            call (serviceSelection (abstractService (WS_i)))
 9:            break;
10:        end if
11:        globalDescription = WS_i servicedescription from Registry
12:        if serviceDescription (WS_i) not equals globalDescription then
13:            remove WS_i from LCS concrete service list
14:            call (serviceSelection (abstractService (WS_i)))
15:            break
16:        end if
17:        currentData = invoke WS_i.operation
18:        if currentData not equals previousData  then
19:            call (ResponseConsolidation (currentData))
20:            break
21:        end if
22:        compare WS_i(description) with Conversation_{metrics}
23:        if not equivalent  then
24:            remove WS_i from LCS concrete service list
25:            call (serviceSelection (abstractService (WS_i)))
26:            break
27:        end if
28:        WS_{optimal} = select "best" WS from Community_i
29:        if WS_i not equals WS_{optimal} then
30:            remove WS_i from schema
31:            add WS_{optimal} to schema
32:            break
33:        end if
34:        LCS_{specification} = listen currentSpecification
35:        if LCS_{specification} not equals null  then
36:            call (generateLCS (LCS_{specification}))
37:            break
38:        end if
39:    end for
40: end while
41: decrement time
```

The algorithm starts by verifying the availability of each Web service by sending alive messages to the Web services in the the LCS concrete service list. If a Web service is not available, it is removed from the LCS concrete service list and an alternate service is selected. Second, the algorithm requires checking for changes in operations. The respective agent retrieves the current description of each Web service from the global service registry and compares it with the description in the system. If the description has changed, the agent removes the service description from the LCS concrete service list and selects an alternate service. Third, the agent compares the contents returned by the Web service with the contents of the previous response. If the agent detects any change, the response must be reconsolidated.

The algorithm verifies the non-functional characteristics of each Web service by comparing the Web service descriptions with the conversational metrics defined by the entrepreneur. If a Web service does not comply, it is removed from the participantList and an alternate service is selected. Second, the algorithm checks for changes in the functional or QoWS attributes.

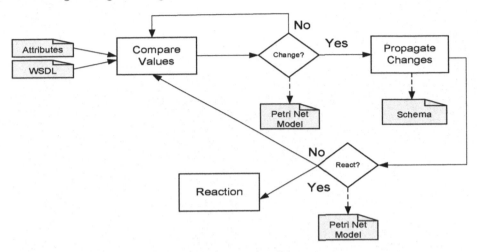

Fig. 7.3 Flow Diagram for Bottom Up Change Management

The *optimal* Web service is selected from the community. The respective agent retrieves the current "best" Web service from the community and compares it with the description in the participantList. If the description has changed, the agent removes the participating service and selects the alternate service. Finally, the agent *listens* for any updates to the LCS specification. If the agent detects any change, the LCS is regenerated.

Figure 7.1: Flowchart of the Change Management System.

The Update Web service is selected from the community. The people frequently retrieve the current "data". Web service from the community and compares it with the data in the particular data set. If the description does not match, it updates/removes the particular data set and selects the appropriate service. Finally, the system checks for any updates to the UCS application. If the system detects any change to the UCS is registered.

Chapter 8
Performance Study

In this chapter, we conduct a set of experiments and simulations to evaluate the performance of the process of change management, including ontology query, top-down change enactment, top-down change optimization, and bottom-up change management. We will elaborate on the performance study for each of them in the following sections.

8.1 Ontology Query

We conducted a set of experiments to assess the performance of the proposed query approach. We run our experiments on a Mac Pro with 2.66 GHz Quad-Core processor and 6GB DDR3 memory under Mac OX operating system.

In order to evaluate the query efficiency, we need to first build a complete service ontology, referred to as $\mathcal{O}$, upon which the query can be applied. We describe the key parameters and illustrate how each of these parameters are used to construct the service ontology. Table 8.1 shows the definitions of the parameters and their values.

8.1.1 Constructing the Service Ontology

We define two key parameters to determine the size of $\mathcal{O}$: depth d and total number of service nodes n. We will evaluate the effect of both d and n on the query efficiency. We construct the service ontology level by level. The construction starts from the root, which is a dummy node with an id of 1, representing the entry point of the ontology. The fanout of each node is a randomly generated number with an upper bound of f. For instance, if the fanout is 3, the root node will have three child nodes, whose ids are 11, 12, and 13. The parent-children relationship has two types: $t_1 =is\text{-}a$ and $t_2 =has\text{-}$

Table 8.1 Parameter Settings

Parameter	Meaning	Values
d	Ontology depth	[5, 20]
n	Total nodes	$[10^3, 10^6]$
f	Node fanout	[5, 14]
k_1	Number of new operations	[1, 5]
k_2	Number of inherited operations	[1, 4]

of. We randomly assign t_1 or t_2 between a child node and its parent. If a child node cn holds an *is-a* relationship with its parent pn, cn will inherent all the operations from pn. In addition, k_1 randomly generated new operations will also be assigned to cn. If cn holds an *has-of* relationship with pn, k_2 operations will be randomly selected from the operation set of pn and assigned to cn. We assign no operations for the root node since it is just an entry point of the service ontology.

We leverage a FIFO queue Q to facilitate the process of building the service ontology $\mathcal{O}$. We start by generating the root node and inserting it into Q. The root node is then extracted from Q. All its child nodes are generated based on the rationale we described above. These child nodes are then inserted into Q. The node generation stops when the depth or the maximum number of nodes are reached. After that, we continue to extract the node from the queue until it becomes empty.

8.1.2 Performance Study

We study the performance of the heuristic query algorithm (referred to as HeuQuery) and advanced heuristic query algorithm (referred to as AdHeuQuery) in this section. HeuQuery assumes that there is no confusing nodes in the graph. AdHeuQuery allows the existence of the confusing nodes. We also implemented a Depth First Search (referred to as DFS) on the service ontology for comparison purpose. By performance, we report both the node accesses (referred to as NA), which is independent of hardware settings, and the actual running time on our experiment machine.

8.1.2.1 Depth of the Service Ontology

We study the effect of the depth of the service ontology in this section. We keep the maximum fanout as 4, i.e., $f = 4$, and vary the depth from 5 to 20. Figure 8.1 shows how the number of node accesses varies with the depth

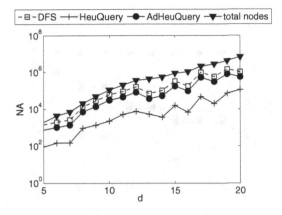

Fig. 8.1 NA Vs. d

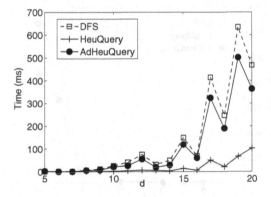

Fig. 8.2 Time (ms) Vs. d

of the service ontology. Generally, DFS accesses more nodes as the depth of
the service ontology increases. This increase is in line with the increase in
the size of the service ontology (in terms of the total nodes). Both HeuQuery
and AdHeuQuery accesses the much less number of nodes than DFS.This is
because they heuristically prune the search space by only picking the *is-a*
children to proceed. Since these two relationships are randomly generated,
they may not necessarily increase with the depth. This also accounts for the
larger performance difference when the depth increases. AdHeuQuery access
more nodes than HeuQuery. This is because AdHeuQuery allows confusing
nodes in the tree. The heuristic search cannot be performed when it hits a
confusing node. Figure 8.2 shows the actual CPU time, which demonstrates
a very similar trends as the number of node accesses.

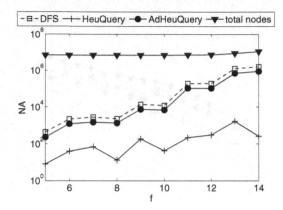

Fig. 8.3 NA Vs. f

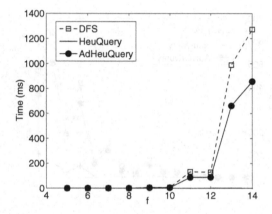

Fig. 8.4 Time (ms) Vs. f

8.1.2.2 Fanout of the Service Nodes

We investigate the effect of the maximum node fanout f in this section. We keep the depth of the ontology as 4, i.e., $d = 4$, and vary the maximum fanout from 5 to 14. Figure 8.3 and 8.4 show the number of node accesses and the CPU time, respectively. The results are fairly consistent with those from Section 8.1.2.1. The results also further confirm the efficiency of the proposed algorithms.

8.2 Change Enactment

We implement a change management system in a Web service environment. The system is designed based on the following three assumptions. First, changes occur in a sequential way. We will deal with concurrent changes in our future work. Within a change specification, there is no requirement on the implementation order between different change operators. Second, we assume that the change requirement is feasible. Put differently, we can always find the Web services that fulfill the functional and non-functional requirements of a change. Third, we assume that a change is initiated from a single user. There should not be any conflict in a change specification. An example of such a conflict is that a change may require to add and remove a Taxi service at the same time.

8.2.1 Prototype

As depicted in Figure 8.5, the system consists of several components, including *User Interface, Change Management, Ontology Support, Web Service Providers, Web Service Registry,* and *Visualization.* We will elaborate on each component in this chapter.

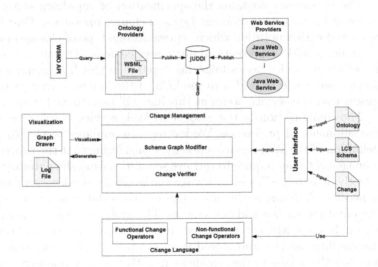

Fig. 8.5 The change management system

8.2.1.1 User Interface

The proposed change management framework uses a graphic user interface to get three types of information as its input: *a LCS schema graph, a change specification,* and *a Web service ontology.* The information is stored as configuration files.

Users need to edit a configuration file graph.dat which contains the definition of a LCS schema graph. The information includes the nodes of the graph and the two sets of edges (i.e., data flow edges and the control flow edges). Each node represents an abstract Web service and is assigned to an id. An example of such a node id is n_1. Each node corresponds a concept in a Web Service Modeling Language (WSML) file, which contains the semantic definition of the abstract service. A data flow edge is represented as a triplet: the node that the edge comes from, the node that the edge goes to, and a data set pair delivered by the edge. An example of such a triplet is $\{n_1,$ $n_2,$ {arrival_date, check_in_date}}, which means that an airline service sends a message to a hotel service containing the information of the arrival_date, which can be used as the check_in_date for the hotel service. A control flow edge is represented as a triplet: the node invoked first, the node invoked afterwards, and the condition on the invocation of the second node. An example of such a triplet is $\{n_1, n_2,$ "true"}, which means that a hotel service will be invoked after an airline service is invoked. The system will first read the graph.dat and initialize the LCS schema graph.

The change.dat contains the specification of top-down changes. We use different lines to store different types of change operators. That is, each line is started with a notation which represents one type of change operators. For example, "op_01" represents adding a service node. Therefore, there will be a set of ids of service nodes following "op_01" in this line, meaning that these service nodes will be added to the LCS. If the line is started with "op_02", it means that the service nodes at this line will be removed from the LCS.

The configuration of the associated Web service ontology is specified in the sub-menu of preference. We leverage an ontology service to provide the definition of the Web service ontology. Considering that the process of change management may require to retrieve semantics from the ontology service frequently, it is not efficient to invoke the ontology service every time when it is needed. To improve the efficiency, we use a database as a cache between the ontology service and the system. The system accesses the ontology service only once when it is started. It will retrieve all the information from the ontology service and stored it in a database. By doing this, the system localizes the access to the semantics in a Web service ontology and improves this efficiency.

8.2.1.2 Ontology Support

In our proposed change management framework, we use ontologies to support the automation of the process of change management. The ontology support includes both *semantic* support and *query* support. The semantic support is to provide machine-understandable description of Web services such that they can be automatically located and orchestrated. The query support is to provide an efficient way to retrieve the semantics from the proposed ontology. In our prototype, we focus on the semantic support. The performance evaluation of the query support will be covered in Chapter 2. We design three subcomponents to achieve semantic support, including *Ontology Providers*, *Web Service Registry*, and *WSMO API*.

A Web service ontology definition is offered by *ontology providers*, which can be some knowledge experts in a certain domain. The definition will be wrapped in a WSML file. A WSML file consists of a set of *service concepts*. Each concept corresponds to a type of functionality offered by Web services in a domain. A service concept defines service properties, such as the service data (i.e., input and output), service operations, quality parameters, and context model. It adds machine-understandable semantics to the description of the properties. For example, for each data item of the input of a service, WSML specifies its definition in a namespace. By doing this, the meaning of the data items can be understandable by machines. More specifically, a WSML file corresponds to a service ontology of a domain. It contains a set of concepts. Each concept defines a type of functionality. A WSML file also contains the definition of the dependency relationships between different services. A dependency relationship is captured as a triplet $\{n_1, n_2, d\}$, meaning that the data item set d is included in the input of the service node n_1 and the output of n_2. n_1 depends on n_2 to provide d.

A service registry serves as a broker between service providers and service users. More specifically, the service providers publish their services to a service registry and service users query and locate their desired service from the registry.

The Web service registry maintains the information of a list of Web services, including their functionality (i.e., the operations they offer) and their invocation (i.e., the endpoints). In the proposed system, the Web service registry also maintains the semantic description of the Web services. When a Web service is published to the service registry, it also registers its mapping to a Web service ontology to the registry. For example, a service may offer two operations: op_1 and op_2. These two operations are mapped to two abstract services in the travel service ontology airline_quotation and airline_reservation. By using this mapping, the semantic description of the operations can be retrieved and understood by machines. The mapping between Web services and a service ontology also improve the service independency. More specifically, service providers are independent with respect to their naming mechanisms for the services and operations and the way they implement the functionality.

We use WSMO APIs to maintain and retrieve the semantics from a set of WSML files. The WSMO APIs provide a Java-based programming interface to build semantic Web service applications. By using WSMO APIs, we can define a set of concepts in term of classes and their instances, such as the data type of the input and output of the a service. We can also define the dependency relationships between different services. These semantic information is defined in WSML files. The WSMO APIs allow the retrieval of the semantics from WSML files. We also use WSMO APIs to implement the Web service registry. More specifically, we use the concept-instance relationship to build up the mapping between a Web service and its subscribing abstract services in the service ontology.

The application modules for this part include the follows.

- **Get_Inputs:** This module is designed to get a list of input data items of an abstract service. It takes a WSML file as input and generates the input data items as well as their formal definitions. The WSML contains the semantic description of a certain type of Web services. For example, airline.wsml describes the properties of Web services that offer the airline reservation functionality.

- **Get_Outputs:** This module is designed to get a list of output data items of an abstract service. It takes a WSML file as input and generate the output data items as well as their formal definitions.

- **Get_Operations:** This module is designed to get a list of operations provided by an abstract service. It takes a WSML file as input.

- **Get_Concepts:** This module is designed to get the formal definition of a term. It takes a term and a WSML file as an input and generates the name of the related concept as output. The term can be an input or output of a service. It should be an instance of a concept that is defined in a certain namespace.

- **Get_Instances:** This module is designed to get the instances of a concept. It takes a concept and a WSML file as an input and generates a set of instances of the concept as output. An instance can be either a data item or a service. For the formal case, the output of this module will be a set of data items that have the same meaning, such as zipcode and postcode. For the latter case, the output of this module will be a set of wsdl URIs that refer to a set of Web services that provide the similar functionality.

- **Check_Dependency:** This module is designed to check the dependency between two services. It takes two service Ids as input and generate a set of data items. If there is a dependency relationship between these two services, the output of this module will be the data items that are associated with the relationship. If not, the module returns an empty set.

8.2.1.3 Change Management

The system focuses on managing changes at the schema-level. It is mainly performed for the purpose of fulfilling the functional requirement of changes. Since we use a graph to define the functionality of a LCS, the graph will be modified once there is a requirement to change the functionality of LCSs. The two types of correctness of a LCS schema graph need to be maintained: semantic and structural correctness. Therefore, there are two subcomponents implemented for this phase: *schema graph modifier* and *change verifier*.

The schema graph modifier maintains and manages the schema graph of a LCS. A graph contains a set of service nodes. Each node is associated with a WSML file, where the semantic service definition is stored. The data flow and control flow among different services are stored in terms of two edge sets in the graph. The schema graph modifier takes a change operator as input, such as *adding a service node* and *removing a service node*. It first checks whether the change is feasible. If yes, it then implements the algorithms proposed to modify the graph to implement the change operators. We use Java to implement this part. The application modules for this part include the follows.

- **Schema_Graph_Initialization:** This module is designed to initialize a LCS schema graph. It first reads the configuration file graph.dat which contains the description of the schema graph. It then uses the information to assign values to the graph's elements, including the nodes and two sets of edges.
- **Change_Analysis:** This module is designed to generate a set of steps of change reaction. It first reads the configuration file change.dat which contains the description of the changes. It then calls other modules to implement the changes.
- **Update_Inputs:** This module is designed to change the user input of a LCS. The input data items that are intended to be added are stored in an arraylist AddInputs. The input data items that are intended to be deleted are stored in an arraylist RemoveInputs.
- **Update_Outputs:** This module is designed to change the abstract services that a LCS outsources. It will first add service nodes to the LCS schema graph. The information about these service nodes is stored in an arraylist AddServices. It will then remove services from the LCS schema graph. The information about these service nodes is stored in an arraylist RemoveServices.
- **Update_AbstractServices:** This module is designed to change the abstract services that a LCS outsources. It will first add service nodes to the LCS schema graph. The information about these service nodes is stored in an arraylist AddServices. It will then remove services from the LCS schema graph. The information about these service nodes is stored in an arraylist RemoveServices.

- **Update_DataEdges:** This module is designed to update the data flow edge set of a LCS schema graph. A data flow edge is represented as a triplet $\{n_1, n_2, d\}$, meaning that service node n_1 sends a message to n_2 containing the data set of d. This module will first map the data transfers specified in the change file to data flow edges and add them to the LCS schema graph. The information about these data transfers are stored in an arraylist AddDataTransfer. This module will first map the data transfers specified in the change file to data flow edges and add them to the LCS schema graph. The information about these data transfers are stored in an arraylist AddDataTransfer. It will then delete the data transfers specified in the change file from the LCS schema graph. The information about these data transfers are stored in an arraylistRemoveDataTransfer.

The change verifier checks and ensures that the correctness has been maintained during the process of implementing a change operators. When checking the semantic correctness, it takes input from a set of WSML files to get the semantic description of a service node. The information required by the change verifier includes service input, output, and the dependency relationship between services. By using the information, the change verifier first detects and fixes the incorrectness of data transfer among services. It then detects and fixes the inconsistency between the data transfer and the invocation order among services. We use Java and the WSMO API to implement this part. The application modules for this part include the follows.

- **Check_Data_Transfers:** This module is designed to check and ensure that all the service nodes can get their required input. It takes a LCS schema graph as input and updates the graph if necessary. This module takes a two-step process. During the first step, it will call the module of Get_Inputs to get the input information of each service. It then compares the input and the related data flow edges to check whether there is any input data item that can not be covered by the data flow. If yes, the service will be added to an arraylist IncompleteInputNodes. During the second step, the module will generate new data transfers for the services in IncompleteInputNodes so that they can get their required input. It will first call the module of Check_Dependency to check whether the service depends on other services to provide the input. If yes, a new data flow edge between the two services will be created and added to the schema graph. If there is still any input data item that can not be covered by the data flow, the module will then check whether the user input contains the required information. If not, the module will check whether the other services in the LCS that can provide the informaiton. It will call the module of Get_Outputs to get the output of other services and compare them with the required input data items.

- **Check_Consistency:** This module is designed to check the consistency between the data flow edges and control flow edges. It takes a LCS schema graph and update the graph if necessary. For each data flow edge, the

module will check whether there is a control flow path between the two
service nodes. If not, a new control flow edge between these two nodes will
be created and added to the graph.

- **Check_Graph Structure:** This module is designed to check the structural correctness of a LCS schema graph. It will first check whether there
  is any isolated node in the graph. If so, the node will be removed. For the
  remaining service nodes, the module will check whether there is a data flow
  path between the node to the user node. If not, the node will be removed.
  The module will also check whether there is a control flow path between
  the user node to the service node. If not, the service node will be removed,
  too.

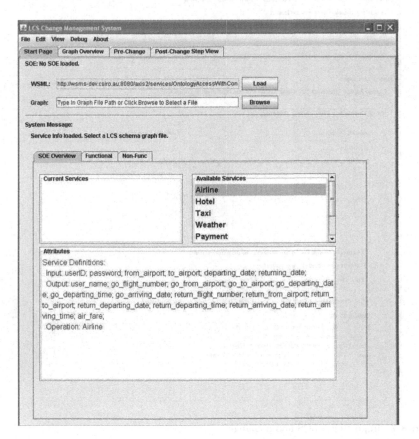

Fig. 8.6 Importing a Web service ontology

8.2.1.4 Visualization

The system provides a graphic user interface for visualizing the process of change management. There are two types of information that are visualized. First, the interface will show the schema graph before and after implementing a change. Second, the interface will show every step of modifying a LCS schema graph, such as adding a node, removing a node, adding an edge, or removing an edge.

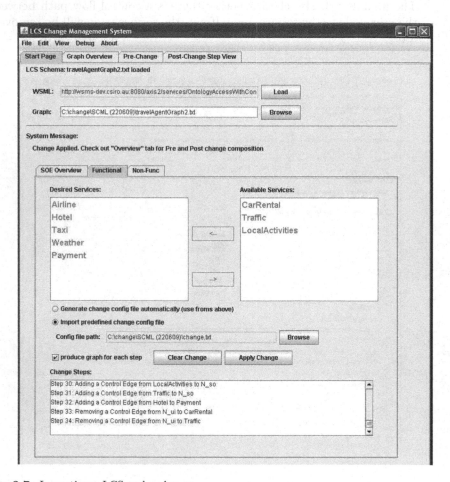

Fig. 8.7 Importing a LCS and a change

For the purpose of clarity, the schema graph is decomposed into two sub-graphs. One sub-graph depicts the control flow among the outsourced services. The other sub-graph depicts the data flow among the outsourced services. A log file is used to keep track of the process of change management. The visualization module reads the management steps from the log file and visualizes them. We leverage the JGraph and JGraph Layout Pro library to visualize the graphs [1]. The graph can be zoomed in and zoomed out for a better view. It can also change the orientation of the graph as required.

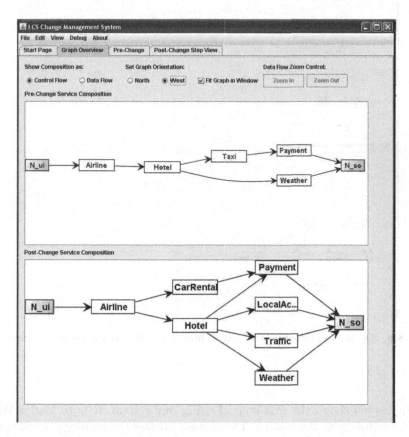

Fig. 8.8 The west-oriented view control flow of a LCS after change management

8.2.1.5 System Usage

In this section, we introduce how to use the implemented change management system. We use a travel agency LCS in our running example as the scenario. For the sake of space, we only introduce some representative steps of using the system.

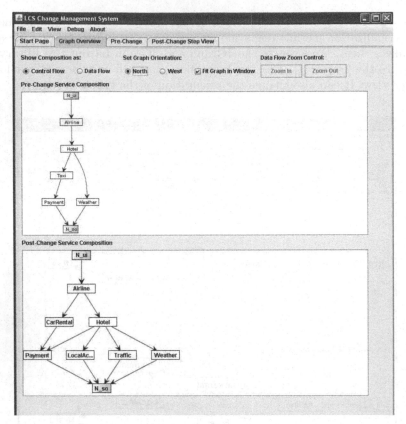

Fig. 8.9 The north-oriented view of control flow of a LCS after change management

Figure 8.6 shows the first step of using our system. It is to load a Web service ontology to the system. The system invokes the ontology service and retrieves the related semantics from the ontology service. By configuring the access to an ontology service, users can import the information from the Web service ontology, such as the types of Web services within a domain and their features (e.g., input, output, and operations.) Users can also import the dependent relationship among services from the ontology to compose services together.

Figure 8.7 shows how to import the information about a LCS and a change specification. A LCS is specified in a configuration file. Once the file is loaded, the user interface will display the list of the services that are included in the LCS. There are two ways of specifying a change. First, it can be done by loading a change configuration file. Second, it can be done by using the left-arrow and right-arrow buttons in the functional change panel. The latter

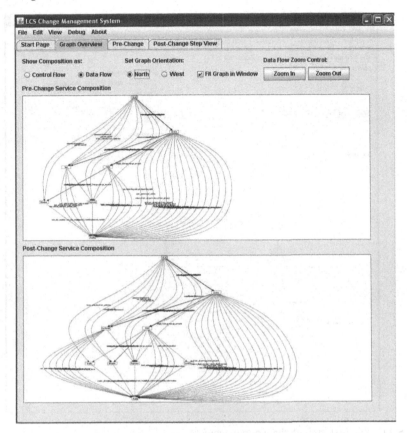

Fig. 8.10   The data flow of a LCS after change management

way can be used if the changes only limit to the changes of the outsourced services, such as adding or removing a service. In this case, the system will automatically generate a change configuration file. It will read the service definition from the database and update the user input and LCS output. Once a LCS schema graph and a change are specified, users can click the Apply Change to implement the change. The user interface also gives an option of tracking the process of managing changes. If users choose this option, the steps of change management will be traced and stored in a file, which can be used for the further visualization.

Figure 8.8, Figure 8.9, and Figure 8.10 show a LCS schema graph before and after implementing changes. Users can choose between control flow and data flow to display the corresponding information. Figure 8.8 shows the control flow of the LCS before and after the change management. In the graph, there are three new services added (i.e.,CarRental, Traffic, and Lo-

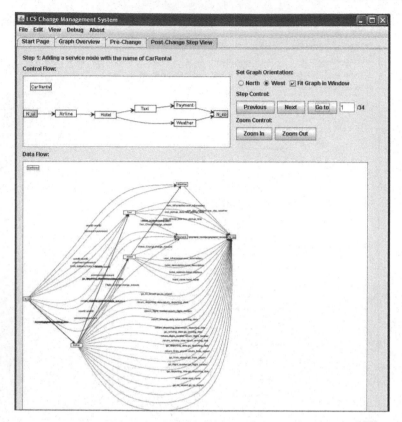

Fig. 8.11 The first step of change management

calActivities). The control flow can also be showed in a different orientation, as depicted in 8.9. The invocation orders among these services and other services in the LCS are automatically generated. Figure 8.10 shows the data flow of the LCS before and after change management.

Figure 8.11 and 8.12 shows the change of the LCS schema graph for different steps of change management. Users can use "next" button to get the difference of the schema graph step by step. Users can also specify a step number and directly jump to the step.

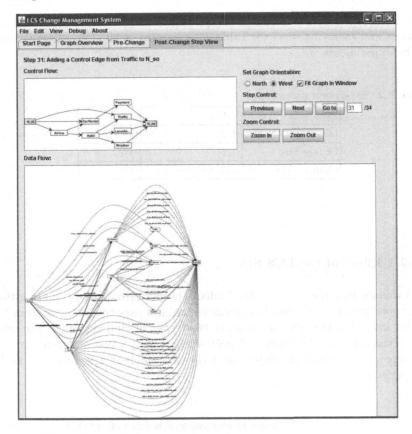

Fig. 8.12   The 31st step of change management

8.2.2 Change Enactment Performance

We conducted a set of experiments to assess the performance of the change management algorithms. We use the travel agency example as our testing environment to setup the experiment parameters. We include typical Web services in the travel domain: Airline, Hotel, CarRental, Taxi, LocalActivities, Weather, and Map. We run our experiments on a MacPro with a Quad-Core processor, 4-GB of RAM, and under Mac OS X 10.5. We focus on three sets of parameters and investigate how these parameters affect the efficiency of the proposed algorithms. In particular, LCS size refers to the number of the services in the original LCS. In the first set of experiments, we study how the LCS size affects the performance. Change size refers to the number of services involved in a change. In the second set of experiments, we study how the change size

affects the performance. We focus on two different types of changes [1]: adding
services and removing services. Table 8.2 summarizes the parameter settings
of the experiments.

Table 8.2 Experiment parameters

Parameters	Values	Symbol
LCS Size	$[1, 7]$	ls
Change Size	$[1, 6]$	cs
Change Type	add, remove	ct

8.2.2.1 Effect of the LCS Size

We evaluate how the size of a LCS affect the performance of the algorithm.
More specifically, we fix the change size as one and vary the LCS size from 1 to
5. We assess the performance against two types of changes: *adding services*
and *removing services*. Since different services may cause different cost for
a change, we conduct the experiment on two different selected services for
comparison.

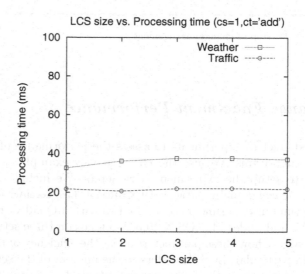

Fig. 8.13 The impact of the LCS size (cs=1, ct='add')

---

[1] Replacing a service can be achieved by first removing the service and then adding a new
service.

Figure 8.13 shows the processing time spent by adding a new service to a set of LCSs with different sizes. More specifically, it presents the time used to react to and verify the change. From the figure, we have the following observations.

- First, the processing time of adding a service does not necessarily increase with the size of LCS. A LCS is assumed to have a correct configuration before a change. Therefore, each service in the LCS can get its input from either the user or the other services. During the change enactment process for adding a service, we only examine the "affected" nodes for the verification purpose. Since adding a service won't cause the deletion of any existing data flow edge, the only "affected" node is the new service. New data flow edges will then be generated to supply the input for the new service. Therefore, the processing time of change enactment does not necessarily depend on the size of the LCS.
- Second, adding a different service will use different processing time for change enactment. Web services are different in terms of service data (i.e., input and output) and their dependent relationship with other services. All of these features have a direct impact on the process of change enactment. For example, suppose service A has more data items in its input than service B. It means that more data items need to be checked when adding service A than when adding service B. Therefore, it is likely that adding service A will cost more time than adding service B. For another example, suppose that service A has dependent relationship with service C in the LCS and service B does not have. Recall that when finding the input supplier for an "affected" service, the service dependent relationship will be first checked. After that, user input will be checked. Finally, if the service still has some input not covered, other services in the LCS will be checked. In this case, C can be first located to provide service A's input when adding service A. For B, in contrast, it may need to go through the entire process to find its input supplier. Therefore, it is likely that adding service B may cost more time then adding service A. As Figure 8.13 shows, adding a Weather service always costs more time than adding a Traffic service since the Weather service has more service data items than Traffic service.

Figure 8.14 shows the processing time spent by removing a service from a set of LCSs with different sizes. From the figure, we find that the performance of change enactment varies when removing different services. When removing an Airline service, the processing time increases with the size of LCS. On the other hand, when removing a Payment service, the processing time varies very slightly with the LCS size. Since removing different services may result in generating different "affected" services, which determines different processing time. An Airline provides input for several services, such as Hotel and CarRental. When removing the Airline service, these services are all "affected". During the change verification process, alternative input suppliers need to be found for each "affected" services. The number of "affected" services is likely to

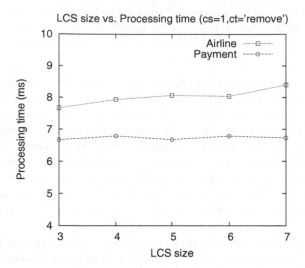

Fig. 8.14 The impact of the LCS size (cs=1, ct='remove')

increase with the LCS size, which leads to the increase of the processing time. A Payment service, on the other hand, does not provide input for other services. Therefore, the processing time of removing the Payment service does not increase with the LCS size.

8.2.2.2 Effect of Change Size

We evaluate the performance in terms of the change size against the LCS size and change type in this section. We set the LCS size as three for the adding services and seven for the removing services. We conduct two sets of experiments which correspond to the two type of changes: *adding services* and *removing services*. We apply two method for adding and removing services. For the first method, the change is applied in a "batch mode". More specifically, when multiple services need to be added to or removed from a LCS, they will be dealt with simultaneously. This method is actually adopted in the proposed change enactment process. For the second method, the change is applied in a "single mode". Specifically, when multiple services are involved in the change, they will be dealt with one after another.

Figure 8.15 shows the processing time spent by adding different number of services to a LCS. The LCS consists of an Airline, a Hotel and a Taxi service. The number of the added services varies from 1 to 4. From the figure, we can have the following observations.

- First, the processing time of adding services to a LCS increases with the change size. Adding services will not cause the deletion of the existing

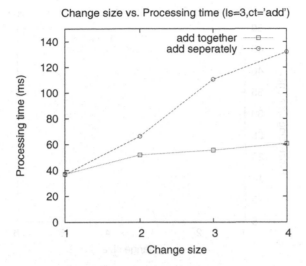

Fig. 8.15 The impact of the change size (lcs=3, ct='add')

data flow edges. Thus, the only "affected services" will be the ones that are newly added. Therefore, the more services that are added to a LCS, the more "affected services" the LCS has. As a result, the more processing time will be used to find input suppliers to these services.

- Second, adding multiple services together achieves better performance than adding multiple services separately. During the process of change verification, once there is a change on the data flow edges, the consistency between the data flow and control flow will be examined. After that, the structural correctness of a LCS schema will be checked too. When adding services together, the consistency and structure check only needs to be performed one time. When adding services separately, on the other hand, the consistency and structure checks need to be performed each time when adding a new service to the LCS. Therefore, it will consume more time.

Figure 8.16 shows the processing time spent by deleting different number of services from a LCS. The LCS consists of an Airline, a Hotel, a CarRental, a Traffic, a Weather, a Payment, and a LocalActivities service. The number of the deleted services varies from 1 to 6. From the figure, we can have the following observations.

- First, the processing time of deleting services from a LCS does not obviously increase with the change size. Removing services will cause the deletion of the existing data flow edges. This may potentially generate the "affected" services. Therefore, it will cost more time on finding the input supplier for the affected services. However, the number of "affected service" does not necessarily increase with the change size. We can use an artificial example to illustrate this. Consider two changes c1 and c2. In c1,

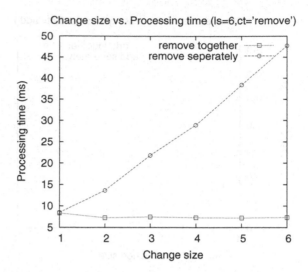

Fig. 8.16 The impact of the change size (lcs=6, ct='remove')

service A is removed. In c2, both service A and service B are removed. Service B is the only "affected" service when removing service A from the LCS. In this case, there are more "affected" service generated in c1 (i.e., service B) than the one in c2 (i.e., none). Therefore, it will cost more time to react to c1 than to react to c2.

- Second, removing multiple services together achieves better performance than removing multiple services separately. The reason is the same as discussed in the case of adding services.

8.3 Change Optimization Performance

We conducted a set of experiments to assess the performance of the proposed change optimization approaches. We assume that the concrete services available to the QoWS optimization process are selected by the reputation manager. Thus the promised quality of these services can be guaranteed with enough confidence. We use the travel agency example as our testing environment to setup the experiment parameters. The purpose is to demonstrate how our approach can help efficiently manage top-down changes in LCSs. We run our experiments on a cluster of *Sun Enterprise Ultra 10* workstations under *Solaris* operating system.

We create a service ontology containing four types of services, including an airline service, a hotel service, a car rental service, and a taxi service. For simplicity, we omit the unnecessary service operations and consider the run-time and business QoWS parameters. Each service contains two operations: $S_{airline}$: (flightSearch, flightReservation), S_{hotel}: (hotelSearch, hotelReservation), S_{car}: (carSearch, carReservation), S_{taxi}: (taxiSearch, taxiReservation). The number of service providers in each service ontology varies from 10 to 60. The values of these QoWS parameters are generated within a range based on uniform distributions. We consider three types of changes, removing a service from a LCS, replacing a service in a LCS with another one, and adding a new service to a LCS. Specifically,

- C_1: Remove the hotel service S_{hotel} from the LCS($S_{airline}$, S_{hotel}).
- C_2: Replace the car rental service S_{car} with a cruise service S_{taxi} from the LCS($S_{airline}$, S_{car}).
- C_3: Add a hotel service S_{hotel} to the LCS($S_{airline}$, S_{taxi}).

We measure the performance of the optimization approaches when applying these three types of changes. We use *computational time* and *score function value* as our evaluation criteria. We conduct a set of experiments for each of the three types of changes.

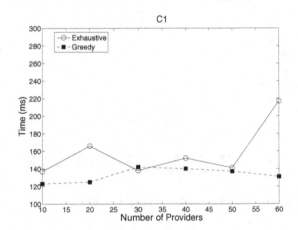

Fig. 8.17 Optimization time Vs. number of providers for C_1

(1) **Optimization time:** Figure 8.17, Figure 8.18, and Figure 8.19 show the total optimization time spent by exhaustive search and greedy search. Specifically, it presents the time used to select the best LCS instance when dealing with changes C_1, C_2, and C_3. For change C_1 where there is one service remained in the LCS after the change, these two optimization approaches have a similar performance. This is because the divide-and-conquer strategy makes no difference when only one service is considered. For changes C_2 and C_3, greedy search is much more efficient than exhaustive search due to the divide-and-conquer strategy.

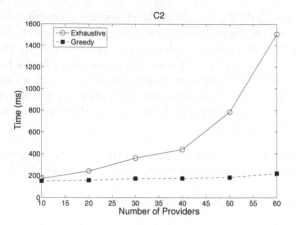

Fig. 8.18   Optimization time Vs. number of providers for C_2

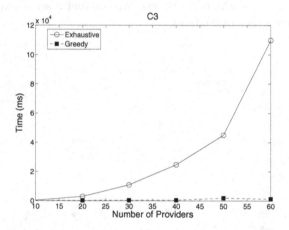

Fig. 8.19   Optimization time Vs. number of providers for C_3

(2) Score of the best LCS instances: In addition to the improvement on the optimization time, greedy search is able to maintain the quality of the best LCS instance. Figure 8.20, Figure 8.21, and Figure 8.22 show the scores of the best LCS instances generated by both optimization approaches. In dealing with all the three changes, greedy search generates the best LCS instances with scores almost the same as those from the best LCS instances generated by exhaustive search. The slight difference comes from the two approximation functions used by greedy search to aggregate QoWS parameters.

(3) Effect of the number of services: In the above experiments, we focus on examining how the number of concrete services affects the optimization time. In this set of experiments, we investigate the relationship between the number of services in a LCS instance and the optimization time. As shown

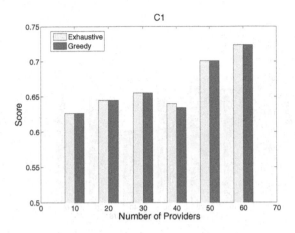

Fig. 8.20 Scores of the best LCS instances for C_1

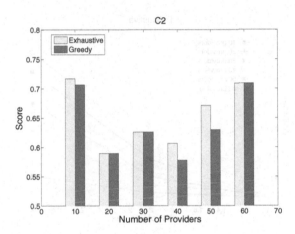

Fig. 8.21 Scores of the best LCS instances for C_2

in Figure 8.23 and Figure 8.24, the optimization time of greedy search has a much slower increasing rate than that of exhaustive search as the number of services increases.

8.4 Bottom-up Change Management

In this Section, we present the implementation and simulation of our bottom-up change management approach. The implementation is conducted in the context of WebBIS (*Web Based Integration of Services*), a prototype for com-

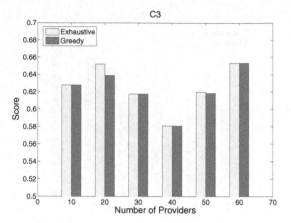

Fig. 8.22 Scores of the best LCS instances for C_3

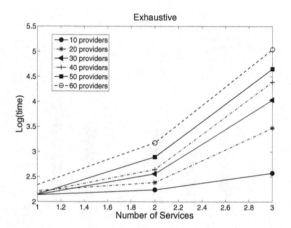

Fig. 8.23 Optimization time vs. number of services for exhaustive search

posing and managing e-business Web services [6]. We use Web services from our travel agency scenario to simulate the changes. We first extend our running example to better fit for the experimental need. We then present the architecture and design of WebBIS. We present our change management framework. Finally, we describe the simulations and their results. We have chosen to perform a simulation study instead of an experimental study because it is difficult to perform change management experiments in a "real" service environment. First, the availability of a large service space can not be guaranteed currently [61]. Second, our aim is to test the feasibility of our change management approach without dealing with other factors (e.g., composition, querying) that may be present in real Web service environments.

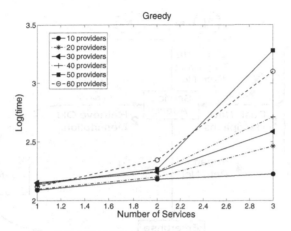

Fig. 8.24 Optimization time vs. number of services for greedy search

8.4.1 Extended Example

We select a change in service availability and execute the change management process in the enterprise. Let us assume that the AA service becomes unavailable. We assume that this change is pushed to the service agent in the form of an OWL-S attribute. When the service agent receives the set of attributes, it compares these attributes with the previous set, which is stored in the local cache. This comparison is based on our Petri net model. Specifically, the service agent compares the new availability attribute with the availability attribute in its cache. The service agent then determines that a valid transition must be enabled. Recall that a valid change transition for service availability is for the attribute to change from available to unavailable. If this transition is detected, we declare that a change has occurred. The service agent *detects* that the availability attribute has changed, indicating that the respective (AA) service has become unavailable. The second step in managing this change is to propagate the information to the enterprise agent. We use the mapping between triggering and reactive changes to determine the propagation of change. The mapping indicates that service availability must be reacted to by selecting an alternate service. Using a publish/subscribe method of change propagation, the service agent will remove the reference of AA service from the enterprise schema. This update of schema indicates that the AA service is no longer part of the enterprise orchestration. Recall that the schema is referenced before any service invocation. Based on this rule, the enterprise agent will check for AA's reference before invoking it. When the agent does not find a service reference, it initiates a reaction to the change. In this case, the reaction is to select an alternate service for orchestration. Hence, a new orchestration schema is created for the ET enterprise.

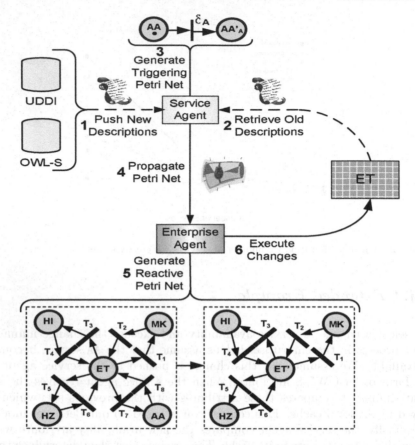

Fig. 8.25 The Flow Diagram for Change Management Algorithm

8.4.2 WebBIS

Our research is an extension to our work on *WebBIS*. WebBIS aims at providing a Web service middleware that enables dynamic and flexible compositions of Web services [6]. The design and development of WebBIS considers two important factors: the use of Web service *standards* for enabling e-business, and the ability to *extend* functionalities of the system. We, therefore, have extended the WebBIS architecture with our proposed change management framework. We have also deployed services from the travel domain that have been referenced in this book. In the following Section, we present the WebBIS architecture. We then focus on the components that are involved in the process of managing changes. Finally, we present the services that are part of WebBIS service space.

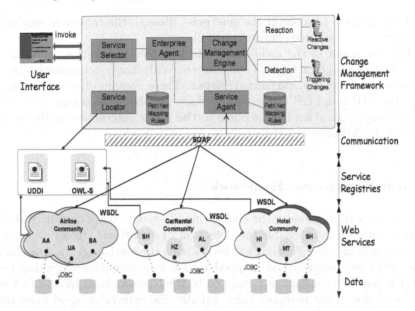

Fig. 8.26 WebBIS Architecture

8.4.2.1 Architecture

Figure 8.26 depicts the parts of the WebBIS architecture that are relevant to our work. The architecture is organized into five distinct layers: *data*, *Web services*, *service registries*, *communication*, and *change management framework*. The data layer consists of a set of Oracle databases that store travel information. The second layer consists of Web services that represent the various travel businesses. The third layer contains the UDDI and OWL-S registries. These registries store service descriptions needed to access our services. The fourth layer represents the communication infrastructure in WebBIS. This layer essentially relies on the SOAP standard for message exchange. Finally, the change management framework layer presents the components required to manage change. It includes components that detect, propagate, and react to changes in the enterprise. Specifically, it consists of the service agent, service locator, service selector, change management engine, enterprise agent, and the Petri net mapping rules. The service agent detects changes to Web services. The service locator looks up services in the UDDI and OWL-S registries. In the change management framework, the task of the service locator is to search for additional/replacement services. The service selector chooses the service that best meets the criteria of the enterprise from a pool of "similar" services. The change management engine processes the change determined by the enterprise agent. The enterprise agent determines the change to be executed based on the information provided by the service agent. Finally, the Petri net mapping rules are used to propagate and manage changes. A

GUI allows users to monitor the enterprise through the change management framework and override changes manually.

The remainder of the architecture displays the communities of Web services and their interactions. There are currently three communities in our architecture: `airline`, `carRental`, `Hotel`. These communities are registered with the UDDI and OWL-S registries. Each member Web service has a local proprietary application that it offers to the users. Interaction in the system uses the SOAP protocol.

Change Management Framework

Our focus is to implement the change management component in WebBIS. This framework must enable the detection of *significant* triggering changes that occur in member Web services by utilizing the service agents. The change must then be analyzed and mapped into a representative triggering Petri net. Changes are subsequently mapped to the business layer by selecting and executing one of the mapping rules. Finally, the enterprise agent must react to the triggering changes. For example, enterprise agent may update local ontology in the event of a change. When reacting to changes, the enterprise agent may abort a pending orchestration of service request (i.e., submitted but not committed or aborted yet) and re-submit it to an alternate member service. This alternate service may have been selected as a reaction to change. We use a change simulator to trigger changes in the service environment. Figure 8.27 depicts the change management framework and change simulator in the context of WebBIS.

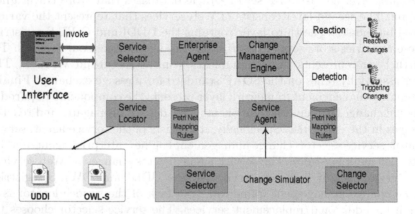

Fig. 8.27 Change Simulator

The simulator is a multi-thread Java application. It has two threads used for triggering functional and non-functional changes, respectively. Each thread pushes a change in a member services to the service agent. The agent updates the functional and non-functional attributes of member services when it receives the notification. The simulator selects the services and the change attribute based on previously known models, such as Poisson and Zipf. To make the simulation more realistic, Java threads are used to synchronize the changes in Web services. The simulator sends a notification message to the service agent. This message consists of a list of change attributes, where the service agent must analyze.

8.4.2.2 WebBIS Services

The WebBIS prototype consists of several Web services from multiple domains. For example, it consists of services from the computer hardware domain (e.g., *Intel, IBM*) and the bookstore domain (e.g., *Amazon, Aracron*). We have implemented several additional Web services in WebBIS to reflect our travel scenario. These include three airline services: *AA* (American Airways), *UA* (United Airways), and *BA* (British Airlines). These services provide the functionality of `getFlightQuote` and `reserveFlight`. We have implemented the hotel service *HI* (Happy Inn), *SH* (Sleepy Hotel), and *MT* (Marot), which provide the `getHotelQuote` and `reserveHotel` functionalities. Finally, we have implemented the following car rental services *HZ* (MegaHertz), *AL* (Alabamo), and *EN* (Enterman). These services provide the `getCarQuote` and `reserveCar` functionalities. Each service is described using WSDL and OWL-S. While we provide the complete description of Web services in WSDL, we limit the OWL-S description to the service profile and the extensible list of attributes. The service profile provides sufficient description for service selection [3]. The extensible attributes represent the state of the the service. They present the functional and non-functional description of a service for managing changes (e.g., availability, reliability).

8.4.2.3 Implementation

The implementation uses state-of-the-art database technologies including Oracle, Informix, and DB2. It also uses Web service technologies, RMI, and database API (JDBC). Agents (implemented using IBM Aglets) are used to detect changes in the system. Web services are described using WSDL and OWL-S. Each service accesses a back-end database to provide the requested service. We generate WSDL descriptions using *Axis's Java2WSDL* utility provided in the *IBM Web Services Toolkit*. These descriptions are published in a UDDI. We implement the UDDI with *Systinet's WASP UDDI Standard 3.1. Cloudscape 4.0* database is used to create the registry for the UDDI. Communication between Web services are encapsulated in SOAP envelopes.

Apache SOAP provides the tools necessary for deploying SOAP messaging. Users access the system through a GUI, which was developed using Java 2/Swing. It consists of two panels. The left panel displays the requests input by the user. The right panel displays all the information returned by the system (e.g., execution results, registration and authorization information). Users may access the system from any Internet host. All information transfers between the GUI and Web services use secure TCP connections.

8.4.3 Simulation

We have chosen to perform a simulation study instead of an experimental study because it is difficult to perform change management experiments in a "real" service environment. First, the availability of a large service space can not be guaranteed currently [61]. Second, our aim is to test the feasibility of our change management approach without dealing with other factors (e.g., composition, querying) that may be present in real Web service environments.

The purpose of our simulation is to prove the feasibility and analyze the performance of our change management approach. The most important factor in our simulations is the *accuracy* of change management. Accuracy (A_T) is defined as the conformity of the reaction to the triggering Petri net generated after change detection. For example, if a change in service availability is pushed by the change simulator, the service agent will generate the appropriate triggering Petri net. This Petri net will be mapped to a corresponding reactive reconfigurable Petri net. The reactive net will reflect the selection of an alternate service, which is the defined in our change mapping rules.

We measure the accuracy of changes in the presence of a *Poisson* frequency. The Poisson distribution is ideal for simulating changes in the Web environment. We use a *Zipf* distribution to select member services that trigger the change. The Zipf distribution is a widely used model to represent the selection of a service from a pool of available services.

We assume that ET is represented as a composition of Web services before changes are triggered. For example, we assume that ET initially consists of the AA, *HI*, and HZ services. These services will then be orchestrated within WebBIS. This composite service is managed once changes are triggered. For example, ET consists of the AA, HI, and HZ member services. These services consist of a getQuote and purchaseTicket operation in the airline service, getQuote and reserveRoom in the hotel service, and getQuote and reserveCar in the car service. These services will be composed and the enterprise will be ready to orchestrate. Any changes to ET after this phase will be managed. Therefore, our fundamental assumption is that ET is represented as a composite service that will be managed during orchestration.

8.4.3.1 Simulation Setup

We run our simulations on a *SUN Enterprise Ultra 10* system with a 440 MHz *UltraSPARC-IIi* processor, and 1 GB of RAM in the *SOLARIS* operating system environment. We utilize only services that offer airline, hotel, and car functionalities. We assume that the Web service space consists of 100 services. Each service has two operations, therefore, a total of 200 operations are present in the services space. Furthermore, each service is utilized by one or more enterprises concurrently. The system consists of two enterprises, ET_1 and ET_2. In our work, we have defined a total of 21 triggering changes. These changes are triggered by the change simulator on behalf of the member services using a *Poisson* distribution. Each round of simulation triggers triggers all 21 changes at *least* once. The total number of changes that are triggered in each simulation are 100. Since each triggering change has a respective reactive change, the total number of reactive changes is also 100. Services that trigger a particular change are selected based on a *Zipf* distribution. Table 8.4.3.1 displays these common settings for all simulations.

Parameter	Setting
Web Services (N_{ws})	1000
Service Ops (N_{op})	2000
Triggering Changes ($\delta(t)$)	100 - 2000
Reactive Changes ($\Delta(t)$)	100 - 2000
Enterprises (N_{soe})	2
Member Services (N_{ms})	1-12

Table 8.3 Simulation Settings

Changes are simulated by the change simulator. The change simulator modifies the functional and non-functional attributes of the member services and pushes the changes to the service agent. Note that we implement a push-based approach for triggering changes. The changes are pushed by the change simulator to the service agent. Also, changes to Web services are represented by changes to service attributes. For example, if service availability change occurs, the change simulator will change the availability OWL-S attribute from 0 to 1. When the service agent receives the new set of service attributes, it compares the new values with the previous values. This comparison represents the change detection phase. A change in any attribute represents a change in the respective member service. The service agent then generates a Petri net to represent the triggering changes. This triggering Petri net is generated by following the rules we have defined in this book. For example, if the service agent detects that AA's availability attribute has been changed from 0 to 1, it will generate a Petri net representing a change in service availability. The rules are referenced from the change management engine. After the triggering Petri net is generated, it is then propagated to the enterprise agent. The enterprise agent maps the triggering net to a reactive net, also using the change management engine. This reactive Petri net defines all the reactions that the enterprise must execute to transition to a safe state. Once the reactive Petri net is generated, the changes are executed in the enterprise by the change management engine. During the reaction phase, we assume that virtual services are already mapped to the concrete services. We select an alternate service randomly without querying for the "optimal" service. For example, the airline virtual service is matched to the concrete AA, US, and DA services. We do not consider any binding constraints for the services. For example, if an alternate service UA is selected, we assume that it can be bound to the enterprise and invoked. After reacting to the change, the control is transfered back to the change simulator. This process is repeated several times during each simulation.

The main focus of our simulations is to verify the feasibility of our approach. *Feasibility* is defined as the execution of change management processes with a *minimum* accuracy. Given N sample results S_1, S_2,...S_N, the minimum accuracy is defined by the constant c. This constant is computed by O/S, where O is the confidence interval half-width and S is the sample mean of the results. Specifically, S is $S_1 + S_2 + \cdots + S_N$, and O is the probability that the absolute value of the difference between S and μ is equal to or less than O. In this case, μ is the true mean of the sample results.

We first measure the accuracy of the change that is detected by the service agent. This detection accuracy A_D is determined by $\sum_{d=1}^{\delta(t)} \frac{A_d}{\delta(t)}$, where $\delta(t)$ is the number of changes triggered and A_d represents the presence of the triggering change Petri net in the triggering set. Each A_d instance is either a 0 or 1. It is 0 if the generated Petri net was in the triggering set and 1 if it was not present in the triggering set. Second, we measure the accuracy of the change that is generated in reaction to the triggering change. The reaction accuracy A_R is determined by $\sum_{r=1}^{\Delta(t)} \frac{A_r}{\Delta(t)}$. Each A_r instance is either a 0 or 1. It is 0 if the generated Petri net was in the reactive set and 1 if it was not present in the reactive set. In our simulation, we use the Zipf to select the service that triggers a particular change. Zipf distribution is well suited for representing words in a text document, book checkout pattern in libraries, incoming Web page requests, outgoing Web page requests, document size on the Web, etc.

We assume that services change by the *Poisson* process. A Poisson process is often used to model a sequence of random events that happen independently with a fixed rate over time [21]. The Poisson process is used to model several random events, including the occurrences of fatal auto accidents and arrivals of customers at a service center. Research has shown that content on the Web follows a Poisson process for change [20, 13]. Therefore, we select each triggering change out of $\delta(t)$ from the triggering set based on this distribution. Table 8.4.3.1 represents the settings for triggering and

	$\delta(m)$
Simulation 1	1:1
Simulation 2	1:m
Simulation 3	m:1
Simulation 4	m:n

Table 8.4 Mapping Accuracy Simulations

reactive change accuracy. Each set of simulation consists of 100 changes in the member services. The number of member services for the enterprise is set to 3.

8.4.3.2 Simulation Results

The first simulation considers the accuracy of change management when a single change is triggered and only one reactive change is required to manage this change. The second simulation tests the accuracy of change detection and reaction when multiple triggering changes occur and require a single reactive change. Similarly, simulation three tests for the accuracy when one triggering change requires the execution of multiple reactive changes. Finally, simulation four tests the accuracy in the presence of multiple triggering changes that require multiple reactive changes. Figure 8.28 depicts the results of these simulations.

The results for the first four simulations indicate that the accuracy of change detection and reaction is 100% if there is exactly one triggering change and one corresponding reactive change. This means that when there is one-to-one or many-to-one mapping between the triggering and reactive changes, our approach results in a perfect accuracy. However, when there is a one-to-many or many-to-many relationship between the triggering and reactive changes, the accuracy drops to 82%. The reason for reduced accuracy is that the change management framework always executes the *first* reactive change indicated by the reactive net. Since 82% of the one-to-many and many-to-many changes require a selection of alternate service, their reaction is executed accurately. For others, the reaction is invalid and does not comply with our change mapping rules. For example, if a triggering change of availability occurs, the reaction is to either select an alternate service, or to execute the enterprise without the service. Since selecting an alternate service is hierarchically above the service deletion reaction, the reaction to service unavailability is always to select an alternate service. In our future work, we plan to prioritize changes and determine a reaction that will result in the optimal enterprise.

The second set of simulations measure the accuracy of change management when the number of triggering changes increases from 100 to 2000. The first

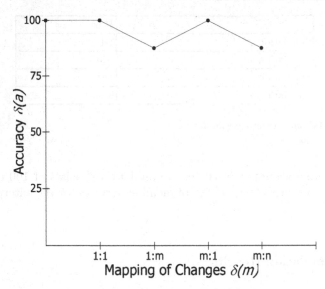

Fig. 8.28 Accuracy for Change Mappings

	$\delta(t)$
Simulation 1	100
Simulation 2	500
Simulation 3	1000
Simulation 4	2000

Table 8.5 Accuracy Simulations for Increasing Number of Changes

simulation in this set measures the accuracy when 100 triggering changes occur. The second simulation tests the accuracy of change management when 500 changes occur. Similarly, simulations three and four test the accuracy of change management when 1000 and 2000 changes occur, respectively. We assume that all changes triggered in these set of simulation have a one-to-one mapping of changes. Table 8.4.3.2 presents the settings for these simulations. Figure 8.29 depicts the results of these simulations.

The results of these simulations indicate a slight drop in accuracy as the number of changes increase. For example, when the number of changes are 100, the accuracy of change management is 100%. As the number of changes approaches to 500, the accuracy drops to 98%. At 2000 changes, the accuracy of our approach is measured at 81%. This drop in accuracy is attributed to the highly volatile nature of ET during change management. First, ET and it's member services' attributes are constantly changing. Because changes occur simultaneously, it is possible that the state of the service retrieved by the service agent is not accurate. Second, ET's membership will change

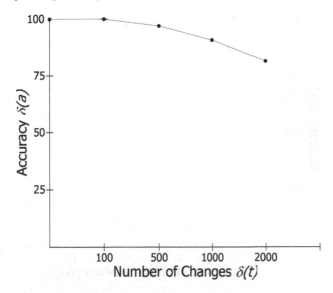

Fig. 8.29 Accuracy for Increasing Number of Changes

	N_{ms}
Simulation 1	1
Simulation 2	3
Simulation 3	6
Simulation 4	12

Table 8.6 Accuracy Simulations for Increasing Member Services

over time. For example, if AA becomes unavailable and no alternate service exists, ET will orchestrate without AA. In this case, any change generated by the change simulator that references to an airline service is inherently inaccurate.

The third set of simulations measure the accuracy of our change management approach as the number of member service increases. We start the simulation with one member service. We then increase the number of member services to three and measure the accuracy. We again measure the accuracy of change management when the number of member services is six. The maximum number of member services we consider are 12. We consider the number of changes to remain constant at 100. Also, the mapping of changes is set as one-to-one. Table 8.4.3.2 presents the settings for these simulations. Figure 8.30 depicts the results of these simulations. The simulations indicate that the accuracy of change management remains optimal when the number of member services is between 1 and 3. However, the accuracy drops to

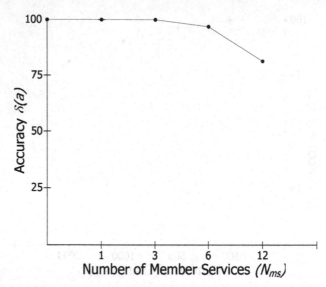

Fig. 8.30 Accuracy for Increasing Member Services

slightly below optimal when N_{ms} is 6. The accuracy further decreases when N_{ms} is 12.

Chapter 9
Conclusion

In this chapter, we summarize the major contributions of this research. We then discuss several directions for the future research.

9.1 Research Summary

Web services are gaining momentum as a new computing paradigm for delivering business functionalities on the Web. They are increasingly regarded as the most promising backbone technology that enables the modeling and deployment of the Service-Oriented Architecture. Many service providers expose to move their business functionalities on the Web using Web services. This, in turn, has opened the opportunities for composing autonomous services on demand. Meanwhile, it has raised the research issues of managing changes during the lifetime of composed services.

9.1.1 Top-down Change Management

We formally define a Web service ontology to capture the common features of Web services in a certain domain. The semantics defined can be used for automatic service selection and composition. Web services are classified into different categories based on their functionality. Based on the classification, we define a tree-like structure for a Web service ontology. Each service category is defined as a service concept in a Web service ontology, a.k.a., abstract service. We also propose a set of query mechanisms for efficiently retrieving semantics from the hierarchical structure of a Web service ontology.

We formally define a LCS schema that gives a high-level description of a LCS. A LCS schema provides the semantics for specifying, reacting to, and verifying changes. The LCS schema is expected to help software agent understand what a LCS offers and how it works. We use a direct graph to define the composition among services. The graph includes two sets of edges, which correspond to the execution order and message exchange among services, respectively. We then define the correctness of a LCS schema based on the definition.

We propose a change management language to specify top-down changes in a LCS. Each change is associated with a requirement on modifying a LCS's feature, both functional and non-functional. We first define a change taxonomy that classifies changes into different categories. The change classification is based on their associated requirement. We define a change operator for each type of changes. Based on the change taxonomy, we propose a change language. The change management language, SCML, consists of three types of commands: definitive commands, query commands, and change commands. The definitive commands can be used to define a LCS schema. The query commands can be used to query semantics from a Web service ontology. The change commands can be used to specify changes.

We present a process of change enactment to implement the changes specified in terms of the proposed SCML language. Changes are reacted to at two levels: schema-level and instance level. During the schema-level change reaction, a LCS schema is modified to fulfill the functional-requirement associated with a change. During the instance-level change reaction, a new LCS instance is generated by selecting and orchestrating Web services that both fulfill functional and non-functional requirement associated with a change. We also propose a process of verifying changes. We first check the correctness of a LCS schema from the semantic perspective. It is for the purpose of ensuring that the services in a LCS can be invoked gracefully. We then check the correctness of a LCS schema from the structural perspective. It is for the purpose of ensuring that there is no isolated services in a LCS. We propose a two-phase process of optimizing the result of change management. There are multiple service providers competing to provide a similar functionality. This results in multiple candidates when generating a LCS instance. During the first phase, We use service reputation as a criterion for optimization. The service reputation reflects the degree of users' confidence on whether a service delivers the functionality and quality as promised. During this phase, the services that have low reputation will be filtered out. During the second phase, we use QoWS as a criterion to choose the best service.

9.1.2 Bottom-up Change Management

We have identified a taxonomy of changes in service oriented enterprises using a bottom-up approach. In this approach, we first describe triggering changes that may occur in Web services. These changes are then mapped to reactive changes in LCSs. This specification of changes is a prerequisite to successfully managing changes in a LCS. We use Petri nets as a change specification tool because they provide a visual representation of changes in LCSs. Furthermore, a Petri net model can be used readily for verifying changes in LCSs.

We have initiated the implementation of our specification on top of Web-BIS [6]. WebBIS is a framework for dynamic integration and management of Web services. Future work includes extending our change management approach. We plan to include a top-down approach to specifying changes. Top-down changes are motivated by the highly dynamic business environment. These changes are usually voluntary, and in reaction to changes in the business environment. A prime application of of top-down change management is to modify LCS membership to increase competitiveness, efficiency, or customer base. Using a top-down approach, we will first analyze the types of changes that are initiated at the business level. We will then translate and map those changes to the Web service level. Another area we would like to delve into is managing bottom-up changes to mobile Web services. Indeed, mobile services have some fundamental differences in the types of changes that they experience.

9.2 Directions for Future Research

Future work for top-down changes can one or more of the following:relaxation on change specification, concurrent change management, and bottom-up change management.

- **Relaxation on change specification** - In this book, the top-down change specification is required to contain unambiguous and sufficient information about a change. An insufficient description of a change may result in a failed change enactment. For example, a LCS owner may want to add a car rental service to the LCS. The choice between invoking a car rental service and a taxi service will depend on customer's travel type, which can be either international travel or domestic travel. In this case, a conditional selection process constraint between the car rental service and the taxi service needs to be included in a change specification. This requirement is imposed on the LCS owner, which requires human involvement and is error-prone. Relaxing this requirement could be an interesting direction for our future work.
- **Concurrent change management** - In this book, we assume that top-down changes occur sequentially. Specifically, there is only one change that needs to be managed at one time. In the real world, changes may occur concurrently and they need to be managed at the same time. A top-down change is always the result of a new business strategy, policy, regulation, or law. It reflects a new requirement on a LCS's functional and/or non-functional features. Therefore, concurrent change management

is needed when there are multiple requirements on a LCS at the same time. Concurrent change management raises several new issues that need to be addressed. The issues include: (1) detecting and reconciling the conflicts between different changes; (2) incorporating and dealing with different priorities on different changes (3) investigating the proper management order among multiple changes.

Future work for bottom-up changes may include one or more of the following: prioritizing changes, changes to service semantics, cascading changes, preserving mapping consistency between triggering and reactive changes, and estimating frequency of changes.

References

1. JGRPAH. *http://www.jgraph.com/*, 2001.
2. Serge Abiteboul, Victor Vianu, Brad Fordham, and Yelena Yesha. Relational transducers for electronic commerce. In *PODS '98*, pages 179–187. ACM Press, 1998.
3. M. S. Akram, B. Medjahed, and A. Bouguettaya. Supporting Dynamic Changes in Web Service Environments. In *First International Conference on Service Oriented Computing*, pages 319–334, Trento, Italy, December 2003.
4. G. Antonious and F. V. Harmelen. *A Semantic Web Primer*. The MIT Press, Cambridge, Massachusetts, 2004.
5. Y. Baghdadi. A Web services-based business interactions manager to support electronic commerce applications. In *ICEC '05: Proceedings of the 7th international conference on Electronic commerce*, pages 435–445, New York, NY, USA, 2005. ACM Press.
6. B. Benatallah, B. Medjahed, A. Bouguettaya, A. Elmagarmid, and J. Beard. Composing and maintaining web-based virtual enterprises. In *First VLDB Workshop on Technologies for E-Services*, Cairo, Egypt, September 2000.
7. T. Berners-Lee. The essentials of a specification. Technical report, W3C, 1999.
8. J. Billington, S. Christensen, K. v. Hee, E. Kindler, O. Kummer, L. Petrucci, R. Post, C. Stehno, and M. Weber. The petri net markup language: Concepts, technology, and tools. In *24th International Conference on Application and Theory of Petri Nets*, pages 483–505, Eindhoven, Netherlands, June 2003.
9. D. Booth, H. Haas, F. McCabe, E. Newcomer, M. Champion, C. Ferris, and D. Orchard. Web Services Architecture. Technical report, W3C, w.w3.org/TR/2004/NOTE-ws-arch-20040211/, February 2004.
10. A. Bosworth and M. K. McKusick. A Conversation with Adam Bosworth. *http://www.acmqueue.org/*, 2003.
11. D. Box, L. F. Cabrera, C. Critchley, F. Curbera, D. Ferguson, A. Geller, S. Graham, D. Hull, G. Kakivaya, A. Lewis, B. Lovering, M. Mihic, P. Niblett, D. Orchard, J. Saiyed, S. Samdarshi, J. Schlimmer, I. Sedukhin, J. Shewchuck, B. Smith, S. Weerawarana, and D. Wortendyke. Web services eventing (ws-eventing). Technical report, IBM and BEA and Computer Associates and Microsoft and Sun Microsystems and TIBCO Software, http://www-128.ibm.com/developerworks/webservices/library/specification/ws-eventing/, August 2004.
12. Marco Brambilla, Stefano Ceri, Sara Comai, and Christina Tziviskou. Exception handling in workflow-driven web applications. In *WWW '05: Proceedings of the 14th international conference on World Wide Web*, pages 170–179, New York, NY, USA, 2005. ACM Press.

13. B. E. Brewington and G. Cybenko. Keeping up with the changing web. *IEEE Computer*, 33(5):52–58, May 2000.

14. B. Burnes. Kurt lewin and the planned approach to change: A re-appraisal. *Journal of Management Studies*, 41(6):978–1002, September 2004.

15. C. Bussler. The role of semantic web technology in enterprise applicatin integration. *Data Engineering Bulletin*, 26(4):62–68, December 2003.

16. F. Casati, S. Ceri, B. Pernici, and G. Pozzi. Workflow evolution. *Data Knowl. Eng.*, 24(3):211–238, 1998.

17. F. Casati, E. Shan, U. Dayal, and M. Shan. Business-oriented management of web services. *Communications of the ACM*, 46(10):55–60, October 2003.

18. F. Casati, E. Shan, U. Dayal, and M-C. Shan. Business-Oriented Management of Web Services. *ACM Communications*, October 2003.

19. S. S. Chawathe, A. Rajaraman, H. Garcia-Molina, and J. Widom. Change detection in hierarchically structured information. In *SIGMOD*, pages 493–504, Montreal, Canada, June 1996.

20. J. Cho. *Crawling the Web: Discovery and Maintenance of a Large-Scale Web Data*. PhD thesis, Stanford University, November 2001.

21. J. Cho and H. Garcia-Molina. Estimating frequency of change. *ACM Transactions on Internet Technology*, 3(3):256–290, August 2003.

22. E. Christensen, F. Curbera, G. Meredith, and S. Weerawarana. Web Services Description Language (WSDL) 1.1. Technical report, W3C, https://www.w3.org/TR/wsdl, March 2001.

23. The OWL Services Coalition. Owl-s: Semantic markup for web services. Technical report, http://www.daml.org/services/owl-s/1.1B/owl-s/owl-s.html, July 2004.

24. The Workflow Management Coalition. *WfMC*. http://www.wfmc.org, 2005.

25. G. Cobena, S. Abiteboul, and A. Marian. Detecting changes in xml documents. In *Proceedings of the 18th International Conference on Data Engineering*, pages 41–52, San Diego, USA, March 2002.

26. M. Conti, M. Kumar, S. K. Das, and B. A. Shirazi. Quality of Service Issues in Internet Web Services. *IEEE Transactions on Computers*, 51(6):593 – 594, 2002.

27. F. Curbera, M. Duftler, R. Khalaf, W. Nagy, N. Mukhi, and S. Weerawarana. Unraveling the Web Services Web: An Introduction to SOAP, WSDL, and UDDI. *IEEE Internet Computing*, 6(2):86–93, 2002.

28. F. Curbera, M. Duftler, R. Khalaf, W. Nagy, N. Mukhi, and S. Weerawarana. Unraveling the Web Services Web: An Introduction to SOAP, WSDL, and UDDI. *IEEE Internet Computing*, 6(2), 2002.

29. DAML-S. http://www.daml.org/services/, 2003.

30. P. Deolasee, A. Katkar, A. Panchbudhe, K. Ramamritham, and P Shenoy. Adaptive Push-Pull: Disseminating Dynamic Web Data. *IEEE Transactions on Computers*, 51(6), 2002.

31. A. Dogac, Y. Kabak, G. Laleci, S. Sinir, A. Yildiz, S. Kirbas, and Y. Gurcan. Semantically enriched web services for the travel industry. *SIGMOD Record*, 33(1):21–27, March 2004.

32. N. Catania (Editor), P. Kumar, B. Murray, H. Pourhedari, W. Vambenepe, and K. Wurster. Web services events 2.0. Technical report, Hewlett-Packard Company, http://devresource.hp.com/drc/specifications/wsmf/WS-Events.jsp, July 2003.

33. D. Edmond, A. Bouguettaya, and B. Benatallah. Formal Correctness Procedures for Object-Oriented Databases. In *Proceedings of the 9th Australasian Database Conference*, Perth, Australia, February 1998.

34. Clarence A. Ellis and Karim Keddara. A workflow change is a workflow. In *Business Process Management, Models, Techniques, and Empirical Studies*, pages 201–217, London, UK, 2000. Springer-Verlag.

35. R. Elmasri and S. B. Navathe. *Fundamentals of Database Systems - Third Edition*. Addison-Wesley, Reading, Massachusetts, 2000.

36. C. Fellbaum. Wordnet an electronic lexical database, 1998.
37. D. Fensel and C. Bussler. The Web Service Modeling Framework WSMF. *Electronic Commerce: Research and Applications*, 2002.
38. M. R. Genesereth. Knowledge interchange format. In J. Allenet, editor, *Proceedings of the Second International Conference on the Principles of Knowledge Representation and Reasoning*, pages 238–249. Morgan Kaufman Publishers, 1991.
39. K. Gottschalk, S. Graham, H. Kreger, and J. Snell. Introduction to Web Services Architecture. *IBM system journal*, 41(2):170–177, 2002.
40. H. Gou, B. Huang, W. Liu, S. Ren, and Y. Li. Petri net based business process modeling for virtual enterprises. In *IEEE International Conference on Systems, Man, and Cybernetics*, pages 3183–3188, Nashville, United States, October 2000.
41. D. Gracanin, P. Srinivasan, and K. Valavamis. Fundamentals of parameterized petri nets. In *International Conference on Robotics and Automation*, pages 584–591, Atlanta, USA, May 1993.
42. T. R. Gruber. A translation approach to portable ontology specifications. *Knowledge Acquisition*, 5(2):199–220, 1993.
43. R. Hamadi and B. Benatallah. A petri net-based model for web service composition. In *Proceedings of the Fourteenth Australasian database conference on Database technologies*, pages 191–200. Australian Computer Society, Inc., 2003.
44. J. Hendler. Agents and the Semantic Web. *Intelligent Systems, IEEE*, 16(2):30–37, March-April 2001.
45. Wilfrid Hodges. First-order model theory. In Edward N. Zalta, editor, *The Stanford Encyclopedia of Philosophy*. Winter 2001.
46. R. Hull and J. Su. Tools for design of composite web services. In *Proceedings of the 2004 ACM SIGMOD international conference on Management of data*, pages 958–961. ACM Press, 2004.
47. Farookh Khadeer Hussain, Elizabeth Chang, and Tharam S. Dillon. Defining reputation in service oriented environment. In *AICT-ICIW '06: Proceedings of the Advanced Int'l Conference on Telecommunications and Int'l Conference on Internet and Web Applications and Services*, page 177, Washington, DC, USA, 2006. IEEE Computer Society.
48. T. D. Huynh, N. R. Jennings, and N. R. Shadbolt. Certified reputation: how an agent can trust a stranger. In *AAMAS '06: Proceedings of the fifth international joint conference on Autonomous agents and multiagent systems*, pages 1217–1224, New York, NY, USA, 2006. ACM Press.
49. RuleML Initiative. *The Rule Markup Initiative*. http://www.ruleml.org, January 2005.
50. M. V. Iordache. *Methods for the Supervisory Control of Concurrent Systems Based on Petri Net Abstractions*. PhD thesis, University of Notre Dame, December 2003.
51. R. Khalaf and W. A. Nagy. Business Process with BPEL4WS: Learning BPEL4WS, Part 6. Technical report, IBM, http://www-106.ibm.com/developerworks/webservices/library/ws-bpelcol6/, 2003.
52. Setrag Khoshafian. *Service oriented enterprises*. Auerbach Publications, Boston, MA, USA, 2006.
53. Markus Kradolfer and Andreas Geppert. Dynamic workflow schema evolution based on workflow type versioning and workflow migration. In *Conference on Cooperative Information Systems*, pages 104–114, 1999.
54. L. M. Kristensen, S. Christensen, and K. Jensen. The practitioner's guide to coloured petri nets. *International Journal on Software Tools for Technology Transfer*, 2(1):98–132, 1998.
55. C. S. Langdon. The State of Web Services. *IEEE Computer*, 36(7):93–94, 2003.
56. D. B. Lenat and R. V. Guha. *Building Large Knowledge-Based Systems: Representation and inference in the Cyc project*. Addison-Wesley Pub (Sd), 1990.

57. Xumin Liu and Athman Bouguettaya. Managing top-down changes in service-oriented enterprises. In *IEEE International Conference on Web Services 2007*, UTAH, USA, 2007.

58. M. Llorens and J. Oliver. Structural and dynamic changes in concurrent systems: Reconfigurable petri nets. *IEEE Transactions on Computers*, 53(9):1147–1158, September 2004.

59. Nazim H. Madhavji. The prism model of changes. *IEEE Trans. Softw. Eng.*, 18(5), 1992.

60. P. Maes, R. H. Guttman, and A. G. Moukas. Agents that Buy and Sell. *Communications of the ACM*, 42(3):81–91, March 1999.

61. B. Medjahed. *Semantic Web Enabled Composition of Web Services*. Ph.D Thesis, Virginia Polytechnic Institute and State University, Falls church, VA, 2004.

62. B. Medjahed and A. Bouguettaya. A multilevel composability model for semantic web services. *IEEE Trans. on Knowl. and Data Eng.*, 17(7):954–968, 2005.

63. B. Medjahed, A. Bouguettaya, and A. Elmagarmid. Composing Web Services on the Semantic Web. *The VLDB Journal, Special Issue on the Semantic Web*, 12(4), November 2003.

64. Brahim Medjahed and Athman Bouguettaya. Customized delivery of e-Government Web services. *IEEE Intelligent Systems*, 20(6):77–84, 2005.

65. D. A Menascé. QoS Issues in Web Services. *IEEE Internet Computing*, 6(6):72–75, 2002.

66. J. Meng, S. Y. Su, H. Lam, and A. Helal. Achieving Dynamic Inter-organizational Workflow Management by Integrating Business Processes, Events, and Rules. In *Proceedings of the Thirty-Fifth Hawaii International Conference on System Sciences (HICSS-35)*, January 2002.

67. OASIS Standard. Web Services Context Specification(WS-Context) Version 1.0. Technical report, http://docs.oasis-open.org/ws-caf/ws-context/v1.0/wsctx.html, April 2007.

68. C. A. R. Olston. *Approximate Replication*. PhD thesis, Stanford University, June 2003.

69. M. Ouzzani. *Efficient Delivery of Web Services*. PhD thesis, Virginia Polytechnic Institute and State University, 2004.

70. M.P. Papazoglou and D. Georgakopoulos. Service-oriented computing. *Communications of the ACM*, 46(10):25–65, 2003.

71. S. Patil and Newcomer E. ebXML and Web Services. *IEEE Internet Computing*, 7(3):74–82, 2003.

72. S. Raman and S. McCanne. A model, analysis, and protocol framework for soft state-based communication. *Proceedings of the conference on Applications, technologies, architectures, and protocols for computer communication*, 1999.

73. R. L. Reid, J. B. Tapp, D. H. Liles, K. J. Rogers, and M. E. Johnson. An Integrated Management Model for Virtual Enterprises: Vision, Strategy, and Structure. *IEEE Engineering Management Conference*, pages 522–527, 1996.

74. R. Reiter. Knowledge in action: Logical foundations for specifying and implementing dynamical systems. Technical report, Cambridge, Massachusetts, 2001.

75. S. Rinderle, M. Reichert, and P. Dadam. On Dealing with Structural Conflicts Between Process Type and Instance Changes. In *Second International Conference on Business Process Management*, pages 274–289, Postdam, Germany, June 2004.

76. S. H. Ryu, F. Casati, H. Skogsrud, B. Benatallah, and R. Saint-Paul. Supporting the dynamic evolution of web service protocols in service-oriented architectures. *ACM Trans. Web*, 2(2):1–46, 2008.

77. E. H. Schein. Kurt Lewin's Change Theory in the Field and in the Classroom: Notes Toward a Model of Managed Learning. Technical report, MIT, https://dspace.mit.edu/bitstream/ 1721.1/2576/1/SWP-3821-32871445.pdf, July 1995.

78. S. Shazia, S. Olivera, M. Maria, and E. Orlowska. Managing change and time in dynamic workflow processes. *International Journal of Cooperative Information Systems*, 1999.

79. R. Tagg. Workflow in Different Styles of Virtual Enterprise. In *Workshop on Information technology for Virtual Enterprises*, pages 21–28, Queensland, Australia, January 2001.

80. J. Twist. *Turning the Web into 'Sushi Belts'*. http://news.bbc.co.uk/2/hi/technology/4421707.stm, April 2005.

81. Y. B. Udupi and M. P. Singh. Information sharing among autonomous agents in referral networks systems. In *6th International Workshop on Agents and Peer-to-Peer Computing*, May 2007.

82. P. v. Eck, J. Engelfriet, D. Fensel, F. v. Harmelen, Y. Venema, and M. Willems. A Survey of Languages for Specifying Dynamics: A Knowledge Engineering Perspective. *IEEE Transactions of Knowledge and Data Engineering*, 13(3), May/June 2001.

83. W. M. P. van der Aalst and T. Basten. Inheritance of workflows: an approach to tackling problems related to change. *Theoretical Computer Science*, 270(1–2):125–203, 2002.

84. S. J. Vaughan-Nichols. Web Services: Beyond the Hype. *IEEE Internet Computing*, 35(2):18–21, 2002.

85. S. J. Vaughan-Nichols. Web Services: Beyond the Hype. *IEEE Computer*, 35(2):18–21, 2002.

86. Y. Velegrakis, R. J. Miller, and L. Popa. Preserving Mapping Consistency Under Schema Changes. *The VLDB Journal*, 13(3):274–293, September 2004.

87. S. Vinoski. Web services interaction models, part 1: Current Practice. *IEEE Internet Computing*, 6(3):89–91, 2002.

88. S. Vinoski. The more things change. *Internet Computing*, 8(1):87–89, January/February 2004.

89. W. Vogels. Web Services Are Not Distributed Objects. *IEEE Internet Computing*, 7(6):59–66, 2003.

90. W3C. Simple Object Access Protocol (SOAP). *http://www.w3.org/TR/SOAP/*, 2003.

91. W3C. Universal Description, Discovery, and Integration (UDDI). *http://www.uddi.org*, 2003.

92. W3C. Web Services Description Language (WSDL). *http://www.w3.org/TR/wsdl*, 2003.

93. W3C. Web Service Semantics - WSDL-S . *http://www.w3.org/Submission/WSDL-S/*, 2005.

94. W3C Group. OWL Web Ontology Language Overview. *http://www.w3.org/TR/owl-features/*, Feb 2004.

95. S. Weibel, J. Gridb, and E. Miller. *OCLC/NCSA Metadata Workshop Report*. http://www.oasis-open.org/cover/metadata.html.

96. WSMO Working Group. Web Service Modeling Ontology (WSMO). *http://www.wsmo.org/*, 2004.

97. L. Xiong and L. Liu. Peertrust: Supporting reputation-based trust for peer-to-peer electronic communities. *IEEE Trans. on Knowledge and Data Engineering (TKDE)*, 16(7):843–857, July 2004.

98. J. Yang. Web Service Componentization. *Communications of the ACM*, 46(10):35–40, 2003.

99. Q. Yu. *A Foundational Framework for Service Query Optimization*. PhD thesis, Virginia Tech, 2008.

100. Qi Yu and Athman Bouguettaya. Framework for web service query algebra and optimization. *ACM Trans. Web*, 2(1):1–35, 2008.

101. L. Zeng, B. Benatallah, M. Dumas, J. Kalagnanam, and Q. Sheng. Quality-driven Web Service Composition. In *Proc. of 14th International Conference on World Wide Web (WWW'03)*, Budapest, Hungary, May 2003. ACM Press.

Index